FLESH and BLOOD

FLESH
and
BLOOD

WILLIAM HANLEY

RANDOM HOUSE   NEW YORK

Photographs by courtesy of NBC Studios

Library of Congress Catalog Card Number: 67-14474

To Patricia,
my sister, with love

THERE is currently within the television industry a mood of ambitious planning. The talk is of better things. Not merely the sort of Better Things that are offered the viewing public on Sunday afternoons to appease the Federal Communications Commission, but plays that will occupy the best possible time periods and that won't necessarily come at the American public on a galloping horse or behind a blazing .38 and a suave smile. The burning question is whether or not television can be better than it is and has been and still sell soap. It isn't a new question, of course; it is one that has been asked in the industry by certain of its members for more than twenty years. But television has seemed to get worse while, presumably, more and more soap crosses the counters. This time, however, there is about the question—if I judge correctly—a greater sense of urgency, with the promise, if not the guaranty, of positive results.

My own hopes for a better future for good theatre in television are not entirely unselfish, of course. Certainly as a playwright I want to see people moved, *provoked* to some response, left with the effect of a theatrical experience, an effect that has duration beyond the time it takes for them to reach the top of the aisle after the curtain comes down. But, beyond the possibility of that experience for others—which exists and may be realized *wherever* a play may be performed—television offers the writer two of the necessities he must have in order to survive as a writer: an audience and money. And, in ordinary circumstances, the former breeds the latter. Unfortunately, the audience for serious drama on Broadway has dwindled to a faint trickle. In the 1965–66 season, a reasonably representative season among recent ones, some twenty plays opened on Broadway that could fairly be called dramas: no singing, no dancing, not too many laughs. Many, the majority of them perhaps, were not good plays and were cried out as such by the critics; they closed quickly. But there were favorable, in some cases glowing, reviews for a number of those plays, despite which only two of them were still running at the season's end and neither of those survived the summer that followed. If even favorable reviews of first-rate plays fail to assure an audience, then the writing is on the wall and, as the song says, it spells trouble. Aside from Broadway there are two other areas that must be fairly considered in this pursuit of an audience. The off-Broadway audience potential is no better, relatively speaking, than it is uptown: the theatres are small and even with a respectably long run the playwright cannot hope to make a living from it. The amateur theatre in America, vast and, in certain cases like the American Playwrights Theatre, lucrative as it may be, presents some severe limitations in respect to the realization of the author's intent. The people involved in the productions are, after all, amateurs; a first-rate production might happen occasionally somewhere but, for the most part, the playwright must be prepared to accept questionable results.

So, television then. Certainly there are plays that will never be performed on television, and we who write them will continue to take our chances, as usual, in the theatre, dreaming of that five-hundredth performance. But what of the plays that *can* be done, without serious tampering and with, still, a great deal of risk on the part of the networks? The television audience is so vast as to make any playwright's vision blur; and the money is available too. The question, then, is whether or not places can be made, regularly and consistently, somewhere during the uncounted number of hours of television programing, the best hours, for writers of talent and purpose. To hope for an artistic earthquake would be unrealistic. But there are enough original dramas scheduled for television production in the near future to at least hold out hope for a significant alteration in the landscape. Perhaps they don't all have happy endings, and perhaps the American public will survive them anyway, and perhaps, who knows, the sponsors will even make a little money on them. It remains for those executives in the television industry with some vision and the power to exercise it to find that best time and place for the best work of talented people. And, in order to prove anything, it must be presented not merely as the occasional special event but, I repeat, regularly and consistently for a reasonable period of time. Only then will a true evaluation of the public response to this kind of television theatre be possible. It is surely the only way to make a permanent break from the sort of lowest-common-denominator principle of creative activity that has dominated television programing for so many years.

I've made much of the writer's audience and remuneration as they apply to television. There is, of course, a third crucial requirement for the writer; more crucial, perhaps, than the others, for without it the others lose their significance. I refer, naturally, to the freedom of the writer to write what he will. No discussion of the future of television can evade the matter of censorship. In the case of *Flesh and Blood* censorship was a problem, but not nearly to the extent I had anticipated when the question of its television production first arose. It was suggested by the network that the play contained a number of words and phrases (thirty-four, to be precise) that could not, under any circumstances, be uttered on television since profanity is forbidden by regulations of the Federal Communications Commission. If we could agree on these the play could be done. All but three of the objections were the more or less commonplace vernacular references to the deity considered to be blasphemous. So the censorship had to do with color, not content. A character might say "damn" so long as he did not suggest that God do the damning. And he could say hell almost as much as he damned pleased. Once over the hurdle of these minor excisions, promises were made: the play would otherwise be done as written, the story and the incidents that go into the telling of it were to remain untouched. And, in principle, the promises were kept; the principle here being the willingness of NBC to take a chance, to do something that would surely offend a great many people. But the enemy was time. Two hours were alloted for the production and, allowing time for some twenty minutes of commercials, station breaks and credits, the play had to be cut—cut more drastically than anyone involved, myself included, had imagined would be necessary. So it is important for anyone who sees the production and reads the text to know that those portions of the play that were absent in the production and are restored here were victims of the clock, not the censor's scissor.

Those individuals directly involved in and responsible for the television production of *Flesh and Blood* are identified and credited elsewhere. But I want to extend special thanks to David Tebet of NBC, whose professional devotion to the project—in many instances certainly far beyond the call of duty—was exceeded only by his personal kindnesses; and to William F. J. Storke, who initiated the project at NBC, whose belief in its possibilities never wavered and who, I suspect (although he has never so much as hinted at it), laid more on the line and thereby faced more of a personal risk than anyone else concerned. If this particular play does not attract that immense audience necessary for "success" in television, it may be that Bill Storke stopped at the wrong station this time; but he's on the right track. It would be well for a good many others in the television industry to join him on it.

W.H.
November 1967

FLESH AND BLOOD *was first presented by NBC-TV on*
January 26, 1968, with the following cast:

(In order of appearance)

HARRY	Edmond O'Brien
DELLA	Kim Stanley
JOHN	E. G. Marshall
FAYE	Kim Darby
NONA	Suzanne Pleshette
HOWARD	Robert Duvall

Produced and Directed by Arthur Penn
Unit Manager Bruce Bassett
Asssociate Director Hal Venho
Assistants to the Producer Joan King and Lucy Antek
Scenic design by Warren Clymer
Costume Designer Noel Taylor
Technical Director O. Tamburri
Lighting by Philip Hymes

FLESH and BLOOD

The Set

Three rooms of a six-room apartment near Third Avenue in the Yorkville section of New York City; and the roof of the building.

The living room, the largest of the three, is center stage. In the center wall of the room, a double door, with mullioned windows and curtained, opens onto the hallway of the apartment. To the left of the door there is a false fireplace; on the mantel, a rather ornate clock, somewhat baroque in design; on the wall above the mantel, prominent, a portrait of a young man in an Army uniform. In the corner of the room, there is a Christmas tree, two weeks old, wilting dispiritedly; its lights, initially, are unlit. On the right wall there is a small upright piano, somewhat battered. Downstage of the piano is the door to the kitchen, a swinging door. Downstage center are a sofa, chairs and a coffee table. Downstage, at the furthermost limit, a portable television set stands on the floor, its back to the audience.

The kitchen is a bright room with table and chairs and the usual appurtenances; a window is in the right wall.

A small bedroom occupies the left of the stage. It is sparsely furnished: a bed, a chair, a night table, bureau and a large wooden wardrobe cabinet. Downstage left is the door to a bathroom. Upstage left is the door to a closet. In the upstage wall, at the far right, is the entrance to the room from the hallway. There are many books in the room. The walls are virtually covered with framed photographs, several apparently cut from magazines, magazine covers, and other memorabilia. Also on the walls are several crucifixes of various and unusual design.

3

The hallway is partially seen through the open doors in the living room; it runs the length of the apartment behind the living room, the one visible bedroom, and beyond. The entrance to the apartment, not visible, is at the end of the hallway.

The apartment is old but very well cared for. There is nothing remarkable about the furnishings, but it can be seen that someone with taste and some sense of style has had a hand in it.

The first night. The curtain rises on darkness below; above, snow falls on the roof of a city building and has mounded along the top edge of the parapet. Below the parapet there is a row of windows, dark, and marked with wide crosses of white paint; several of the panes are smashed. In the background a somewhat taller building rises, and its windows too are dark and crossed. There is the air of the derelict and deserted about this place. But beyond it, in the far background, there rises the steel skeleton of a sky-scraper under construction; and to the right and left, the shining glass and marble façades of new structures.

Below in the apartment, light begins to grow. It reveals first HARRY, *a tall, powerfully built man, fifty-nine years old. He wears rumpled corduroy trousers, a dark wool shirt and heavy bridgeman's shoes.* HARRY *is a man of no little sensitivity and perception, but one who has spent his life at callings in which sensitivity and perception have been always less operable than a native shrewdness, a loud voice and a strong arm; until, finally, these latter are the dominant characteristics and the others must often struggle into the light of exposure. He faces directly front now, perfectly still, a bottle of beer dangling from one hand, and is dis-covered, gradually, to be standing in the living room. The television set is lit but soundless. At the right, far downstage and gleaming, is a wheelchair of stainless steel.*

The light continues to swell until the kitchen is visible. Seated at the table is DELLA. *She is fifty-eight, a woman in whose face and bearing there is a great dignity; and in whose eyes there is the profound, perhaps painful silence of*

5

unspoken knowledge. She too is still. Behind her a boiling kettle, standing on a burner turned low, whistles, whispers, quietly, faintly.

The light spreads to reveal JOHN *in his room, a man of fifty-six with an astringent wit; of middle height, lean and very hard. He wears the trousers and vest of a dead-black suit, a white shirt, spotless and starched, and carpet slippers. He wears rather old-fashioned eyeglasses, round and steel-rimmed. The doors to the closet and storage closet stand open; the storage closet, particularly, seems crammed to overflowing with the accumulation of years. On the bed are two suitcases, open and partially packed. There are several cardboard cartons packed with magazines and old newspapers. A small steamer trunk is open on the floor. A number of blank, clean spaces on the walls testify to recently removed picture frames.* JOHN *is seated on the edge of the bed, gazing at a framed picture in his hands. In him, as in the others, there is the stillness—as though to move, other than very carefully, would be to risk shattering, flying apart.*

JOHN *places the picture beside himself on the bed, reaches into a carton at his feet and extracts a small pile of old ten-inch phonograph records. From within the pile a smaller disk falls to the floor: it is the sort of record one makes in booths at amusement parks. He picks it up, inspects the label curiously, and moves to a small phonograph on the bureau; he places the record on the turntable. The sound is muffled, as though heard through the imaginary wall that separates him from the others. But a moment after it commences, both* HARRY *and* DELLA *stir and listen. The record is of poor quality, scratched, but the voices are clearly distinguishable: two men and a woman singing "I Don't Want to Set the World on Fire."* JOHN *listens for a moment or two, then switches off the machine, sits, and becomes still again.*

HARRY *drinks from the bottle. In the kitchen,* DELLA *rises, goes to the stove, prepares tea, and leaves the kitchen. As she crosses the living room,* HARRY *drinks again from the bottle. Nothing passes between them. She passes into the hallway and reappears at the open door to* JOHN's *room. His back is to her and it is a moment before she speaks.*

DELLA   I've made some tea, if you want it.
(JOHN *is mildly startled, and when he answers he does not turn fully to face her*)

JOHN   Yes. Fine. (*She waits a moment, seems about to speak again, then starts away; his voice stops her*) When do you go for Nona?

DELLA   I just called the airport, everything's still delayed. Until the snow lets up.

JOHN   Ah.

DELLA   We'll go soon. (JOHN *nods.* DELLA *moves away down the hall and into the living room. She looks this time at* HARRY, *then moves to the Christmas tree and turns on the lights. She touches the tree as the clock on the mantel begins to chime*) Dry. (HARRY *turns to look as acknowledgement, but does not speak.* DELLA *starts toward the kitchen and stops at the wheelchair*) Did you fix it?

HARRY   Mm.
(*She inspects one of the wheels, rolls the chair a bit, testing; then she pushes it across the room and places*

7

it next to the hall door. She turns and starts back to the kitchen)

DELLA   There's tea.
(She enters the kitchen as JOHN *takes up the picture again, looks at it, and leaves the room, carrying the picture. In the living room the clock continues to chime and it becomes evident that it does not stop even at twelve, but continues on as* HARRY *turns to gaze at it, a slow take. The clock finally stops chiming as* JOHN *appears at the living room door)*

HARRY   *(To the kitchen)*   This goddam clock just chimed about sixteen times!

DELLA   It has to be fixed again.

HARRY   Well, *certainly* it has to be *fixed,* woman, I *know* it has to be *fixed!* *(Turns to* JOHN*)* Sixteen times!

JOHN   So it's sixteen o'clock, Harry, what's your problem?
*(*HARRY *is not amused)* Look what I found.
(He goes to HARRY, *hands him the picture.* HARRY, *looking, merely grunts. There is a pause.* JOHN *watches him for a moment before his eye falls on the lit but soundless television set. He goes to it, bends to the dials)*

HARRY   Leave it.

JOHN   Why don't you turn the sound up, then?

HARRY   *(Sharp, a statement, not a question)*   If I wanted to turn the bloody sound up I'd *turn* it up, wouldn't I.

8

(There is a pause. JOHN *gazes a moment, enigmatic, unintimidated, at* HARRY; *then he turns away and moves into the kitchen.* HARRY *slumps into the sofa, takes another pull at the bottle and gazes at the silent television screen. In the kitchen* DELLA *is pouring the tea)*

DELLA   Are you packed?

JOHN   No.
(She moves to the kitchen door and speaks into the living room)

DELLA   Won't you have something?

HARRY   No, thanks.

DELLA   Please, Harry, you've had no supper.

HARRY   He was a good boy, Del, talent, he was good up there.

DELLA   I know.

HARRY   He would've been one of the best.

DELLA   I know.

HARRY   How do you know?

DELLA *(Gently)*   You've told me, love.

HARRY   Eighteen stories. *(Snaps his fingers)* In pieces all over the street. Pieces. *(Calling out)* He was a good boy, John! But crazy! Like you and me once! Remember,

9

John-o? *(In the kitchen,* JOHN *hears but is mute)* He remembers . . . He was that close to me . . . *(He reaches out a hand, gauging a remembered distance)* But I missed him . . . Eighteen stories.

DELLA   It wasn't your fault, love.

HARRY   I know it wasn't my fault! Who said it was my fault! It was *his*! Stupid kid takin' too many chances! I *told* him! I *told* him, didn't I?
(Pause)

DELLA   Why don't you get cleaned up before we go for Nona.

HARRY   I don't have to get cleaned up for Nona, she knows what her old man is, she don't mind the dirt under my fingernails. *(Abruptly soft)* It'll be good to see her again, won't it, Del? Hah?

DELLA   Yes.

HARRY   We're all gonna be together again. *(Calling out, harsh again)* But where's the point, right, John? Where's the point? *(There is no response from* JOHN*)*

DELLA   I've saved you some supper when you want it.
(She turns again into the kitchen, passing JOHN*, seated at the table. He has the cup to his lips when his hand jerks. He puts the cup down quickly with a clatter and grips the edge of the table, his knuckles white, his body rigid.* DELLA *turns to see him so, and moves swiftly: from a box on a shelf she takes a small*

disposable hypodermic syringe, tears the paper wrap-
ping from it; takes a small bottle of fluid from the
shelf, fills the syringe. She brings a bottle of alcohol
and a small package of cotton-wool to the table and
is about to uncap the bottle)

JOHN   Never mind that!
(He reaches for the hypodermic; she pushes his hand
aside and makes the injection herself in his forearm,
quickly, expertly. HARRY *steps into the kitchen in*
time to see this. He stands watching, impassive.
DELLA *waits, anxiously, until finally the tension*
leaves JOHN's *body and he nods)*

DELLA   All right?
*(*JOHN *grunts an affirmative)*

HARRY *(Quietly)*   That's the second one in three days.

JOHN *(Tight)*   I can count, Harry.

HARRY *(Awkwardly)*   Listen, John . . . I'm sorry about . . .
about being so . . . sharp with you there before.

JOHN   Goddamnit, Harry, knock it off! *Don't pity me!*
(There is a moment of silence and perfect stillness;
in HARRY *there appears to be the same enigmatic*
acceptance of the outburst as there has been in JOHN
at HARRY's *harshness moments earlier.* HARRY *turns,*
finally, and leaves the kitchen; he crosses the living
room and exits into the hall. DELLA *takes the prescrip-*
tion bottle from the table)

DELLA   What about this? *(He looks questioningly at her)*
It's almost finished, you should renew the prescri—

JOHN It'll be enough. (*There is silence*) Any luck today?

DELLA No.

JOHN Are you trying?

DELLA (*Sharply*) I go out every day, don't I?

JOHN But are you trying? (*She evades his steady eyes, moves to the window*) Are you going to wait till they move you into the street? They will. He can't fight it forever.

DELLA I remember the first time I stood at this window and watched a train go by on the El, that dreadful racket, and everything shuddering and the dishes falling into the sink. This place was so shiny-new then. Happy times, weren't they? Simple. Life was simple and happy then. (*She smiles*) Well, at least we've had a few years without the El. When they took the El down that was the beginning of the end, don't you think?

JOHN Get him out of here, Della, it's a dead house. Find a new place. This—this is over, it's all over.

DELLA (*Sharply*) Not for him!

JOHN What about *you*, don't *you* want anything?

DELLA (*After a moment, smiling, evasively perhaps*) I've always been easily satisfied, you know that.

JOHN Easily *persuaded* to be.

DELLA It's all the same, isn't it?

JOHN   To him, maybe.

DELLA *(Simply, a fact, as the cup in her hand is a fact)*   He's
my life.
   (Silence)

JOHN   You'll take good care of Faye, won't you, Del.
   *(She looks slowly at him; it lasts a moment; she
   looks slowly away)*

DELLA   As we always have.

JOHN   You know what I mean.

DELLA *(After a moment)*   I can't be any more to her than
I've ever been. Nor can Harry. A mother. A father. It
doesn't change anything, you see, what you know now.

JOHN   I take what I know with me and all is as before, hah?

DELLA *(Incontrovertibly)   Yes. (Pause. She seems to be
waiting for a word, a sign of agreement; none comes)* It
was a mistake, telling you, wasn't it.

JOHN   No!

DELLA   I think I regret it now.

JOHN   Don't regret it. You were right. You did what you
intended, you gave me something. Even if I can't . . .
claim it.
   (She looks sharply at him)

13

DELLA (*Cold*)   I never thought it might occur to you to do that. To want to do that. Apparently it has.

JOHN   In eighteen hours I'll be gone from here, far from temptation.

DELLA   You shouldn't be tempted at all!

JOHN   Suppose she knew.

DELLA   What?

JOHN   Suppose.

DELLA   *Suppose?* I won't *suppose!* What are you doing! Stop it, do you hear!

JOHN   I'm trying to. I can't.
(*Pause*)

DELLA   I trusted you . . . I trusted you to be able to do for two weeks what I've had to do for twenty years.

JOHN   Can you tell me how to stop wanting to put my hands on what's mine and say it's mine? Can you? At least, you've always been able to do that, Della. She's always been yours, no matter . . . what else.

DELLA   And do you imagine she could keep it from him if she knew? (JOHN *makes no answer, avoiding her eyes*) You *know* she couldn't! She hasn't it in her to deceive! She never has had, you *know* that! She could

never keep it from him if she knew! And what then?
(*A long pause*)

JOHN   You're right.

DELLA   I thought I was doing a good thing in telling you.
I thought somehow that you had a right to know, finally.

JOHN   All right! You're right! I said you're right!
(HARRY *appears, entering the living room, carrying
the empty beer bottle in one hand, shaving himself
with a cordless electric shaver. He wears a clean
shirt and trousers now*)

HARRY   Thatta boy, John! A little noise is what we need,
it's like a *wake* around here! (*He bumps open the kitchen
door and steps into the room*) What's she right about *this*
time, John? (*To* DELLA, *displaying himself*) Better? Look!
(*Shows his fingernails*) Clean? How about a kiss for
clean Harry? (*Grasps and kisses her*) This thing Faye
give me for Christmas really works! (*Strokes his cheek*)
Nice? (*Turns and slams the bottle down on the table*)
Another Dead Soldier! (*Lays the bottle gently on its
side*) Requiescat in pace! Johnny-the-priest will now say
a word or two in memoriam over the remains. (*Gesturing
at the bottle, to* JOHN) Father John?

JOHN   I'll say a few words over your remains in a minute
if you don't watch your mouth.
(*But he has to grin, finally.* HARRY *laughs and throws
an arm around* JOHN's *shoulder*)

HARRY   I'll always say it, John: it's just as well you never
went through with it, you don't have the temperament!
(*To* DELLA) He don't have the temperament! (*To* JOHN)

Am I right? How about a beer then, John?

DELLA Oh?

HARRY Oh, for Jesus' sake, woman, the man can have a glass of *beer*, can't he! What's the difference *now*!

DELLA Harry!
(Pause)

HARRY All right! . . . All right, John, I'm sorry! That was dumb.

JOHN (*Smiling, taking one of the bottles from* HARRY) Come on, let's us have a glass of beer and a laugh.

HARRY Right! Good *Christ,* yes, let's have a laugh.
(John pours while DELLA *glares)*

JOHN Well, he's got a point, Del. Here's lookin' at you, Harry.

HARRY *Right* at you.
(They drink; JOHN *like a man with an old, long-put-away thirst)*

DELLA (*To* JOHN) Is it good? (*To* HARRY) Satisfied?

HARRY Oh, Della! A glass of *beer*!

DELLA It's a start! (*To* JOHN) Does it bring back some memories? It brings back some *wonderful* ones to me, really wonderful.
(JOHN *goes out;* HARRY *follows, speaking*)

HARRY   I often think John was a happier man when he was takin' a little drink now and again. Am I right, John?

DELLA   Oh, for God's sake, Harry, don't be stupid, please just don't be *stupid!* A *little drink!* God!
(She turns away abruptly from the closed door, goes to the window, stands looking out for a moment before she sits at the kitchen table)

HARRY   *(In the living room)*   I don't believe you were ever really an alcoholic, John, I never believed that. What the hell, you just didn't ever know when to *stop.* Right?

JOHN   Well, I suppose you could put it that way, Harry, it's an interesting thought. Original. *(Toasting)* To health, wealth and happiness.

HARRY   And the time to enjoy them. *(They drink;* HARRY *switches off the television)* One thing I always hated about you, though, John, you were always a *sad* drunk. You're my brother, and I love you, but there's one thing drives me nuts, it's a sad drunk.

JOHN   I'll do my best to keep my spirits up, Harry.

HARRY   Oh, but I sure as hell carried you home on my back plenty a times.

JOHN   Often, Harry, yes.
(A thought strikes HARRY. *He looks toward the kitchen door, turns to* JOHN)

17

HARRY (*Sotto voce*) You mind if I ask you something, Johnny? Personal?

JOHN What.

HARRY You been gettin' much lately?

JOHN (*Smiles*) Adequate for my diminished needs, Harry. Why?

HARRY You don't miss the girls too much then, hah? You had a lotta girls in your time, John.

JOHN What's your point?

HARRY (*Hesitates; then, with difficulty*) Well, my point is . . . I think maybe you should've married one of them, John. I've been thinking about that lately, what with . . . what with one thing and another. (*He finishes awkwardly*) I just think you should've married one of them, that's all.

JOHN I think I should have married several of them.

HARRY (*Laughs*) Oh, but we had some good times, though, John! Some *good* times! Remember Frisco? When we finished up on the Golden Gate? That was a time, wasn't it?

JOHN Yeah.

HARRY Oh, a beauty of a bridge! That's one of the best, John, and we helped put it there, right? There wasn't an ironworker could touch you in those days. You should never've quit, you should never've come down, you belong up there, John, like me.

JOHN   Not afraid, I don't belong up there.

HARRY (*Derisively*)   Afraid! What do you mean, afraid! One fall? That doesn't make you—

JOHN   I was *afraid*! (*Pause. His vehemence silences* HARRY) You've never fallen, Harry, you don't know, so don't try to tell me.

HARRY   All right! You were afraid! All right!
    (*He turns away; silence*)

JOHN (*Quietly*)   Don't hate fear, Harry.

HARRY (*Silence;* JOHN *gazes at his back*) That kid today . . . I *told* him to be careful, John, he was taking too many chances, from the day he first come on the job. I *told* him . . . You know who reminded me a lot of this kid? Jimmy Walsh. Remember Jimmy? Went down on the Empire State? (JOHN *nods*) A lot like Jimmy this kid was, chances and stupid tricks. I told him he'd never live to see us top-out on this job if he didn't watch his step. Was I right? Just like Jimmy Walsh. The Empire State. It's like it was yesterday, John.

JOHN   It was longer ago than that.

HARRY   It'll be different around here with you gone.

JOHN   Don't start it again, Harry, okay?

HARRY   We've been *close*, all of us! This's been a close family!

JOHN   Yes.

HARRY (*With violence*)   Well, what in bloody hell are you going back for, anyway! What's there for you now after all these years!

JOHN (*Calmly*)   A hole in the ground.
    (HARRY *glares at him.* DELLA *appears at the door; the two look to her*)

DELLA (*To* JOHN, *still cold*)   Is there anything I can do for you? In your room?

JOHN   No thank you, Del.
    (*She moves toward the hall*)

HARRY   Del? (*She stops*) It's John's last night with us. Can't we have us a good time, all of us, you too, Del?
    (*She looks at* JOHN; *then back to* HARRY, *forcing a smile*)

DELLA   I'm just going to change my dress. Then we'll have us a good time, Harry.
    (*She exits.* HARRY *looks after her, speaks quietly*)

HARRY   That's the only thing that ain't breakin' up, you know it, John? What Del and I have . . . The only thing that ain't breakin' up . . . Maybe you're better off.

JOHN   Yeah?

HARRY   You *have* nothing. No wife, no children, no home

Robert Duvall as HOWARD, Kim Darby as FAYE, and Suzanne Pleshette as NONA.

you can call your own. (*Adds quickly, sincerely*) Not that this isn't your home, John, it is, it's always been that, any time you wanted, but I mean . . . with your name on it. I mean you have nothing anyone can take away from you. You understand what I'm getting at? Everything's breaking up . . . (JOHN *makes no response save his silence*) Don't go, Johnny! Why do you have to go?

JOHN (*In a fury*) I'm going home! Will you get that into your skull!

HARRY *This* is your home! This place! This country!

JOHN (*Wearily*) Oh, this country, this country. Give me your poor, your huddled masses yearning to be rich. Give us a chorus of "The Star-Spangled Banner," Harry. My home is where I came from. I want to go into the ground where I came from. Now, give us a rest, will you, for *Christ* sake.
(*Silence.* HARRY *appears to submit finally, and nods*)

HARRY I'm so angry, John, why am I so angry? You know something? There are days . . . There are days I want to go out into the streets with a machine gun and kill the world. Isn't that an awful thing, John? I was never like that before, was I? Was I?

JOHN No, Harry, you never were.

HARRY I was always a happy man, right? I've loved my life and my work and that made me happy. I've left my sweat in steel from one end of this country to the other and loved it. Remember what Tommy Olson used to say? "Steel is the spine in America's back." Right, John? And

I've helped put it there and it's made me a happy man. (*After a momentary pause*) And I'll tell you something else: I'm still as good as I ever was! In case you've been wondering.

JOHN I haven't been wondering, Harry.

HARRY It was a twenty-three-year-old kid took a dive into the street today, not Harry, not fifty-nine-year-old Harry! Right?

JOHN That's right.

HARRY I'd be no good any place but up there, John, it's where I belong, no place else. One thing I never forget is the year I spent in the mines when I first come to this country, and the cave-in. Buried in the earth for twenty-six hours, with the world pressing down on my skull, wanting to swallow me, and the air getting less and less and less. I belong in the air, Johnny. To be as high in the air as a man can get and still be connected to the earth, that's *something*, John, that's *something* to me. It's where I belong.

JOHN Who says you don't, Harry?

HARRY (*After a moment, abruptly, saying finally what he must say*) I slipped yesterday, Johnny, I fell. (JOHN *frowns*) Yeah. Not bad, I grabbed ahold and hung on till they hauled me up. But I slipped. The first time. I just . . . slipped. (*Pause*) Don't tell Della.

JOHN Listen, Harry—

HARRY You hear? *Don't tell Della.* (*Pause.* JOHN *gazes at*

22

him. DELLA *appears at the door.* HARRY *turns to her*) Del, you look like a million dollars! *Two* million! What do you think, John?

(JOHN *turns to regard* DELLA, *who summons up a smile from somewhere and poses. She is wearing a bright new dress, a party dress*)

JOHN   A veritable flower.

HARRY   Class! Right? It's what I always say: what Della has is *class!* Like a million dollars.

DELLA (*A reminder*)   Two million.

HARRY   Could you be persuaded to have something a little stronger than the usual? For old times' sake? For any sake?

DELLA   The usual. (*Resigned, he shrugs at* JOHN *and goes off into the kitchen. She speaks quietly*) Don't tell me what?

JOHN   What he got you for your birthday.
(*She recognizes the lie for what it is as* JOHN *reaches for the bottle*)

DELLA (*Intense, sotto voce*)   For God's sake, will you stop! (*She seizes the beer bottle from the table; his hand flashes out and grasps her wrist. They freeze, glaring at each other. Finally, she relents.* JOHN *releases his hold on her. She replaces the bottle, turns away abruptly and moves to the chair; takes up the picture from it in order to sit as* HARRY *emerges from the kitchen carrying a glass with ice cubes and a bottle of ginger ale*)

23

HARRY   What about that, Del? Johnny dug that out. Remember? That was our first car, that old Ford. (*Hands*
DELLA *the glass, taps the picture, smiling*) You had a lot
more hair in those days, John.

JOHN   I had a lot more everything.

HARRY   Sharp. You were a very sharp dresser then. Of
course, lately, I don't know, John, you're lookin' like
somethin' outta the Kremlin.

JOHN   Fella down at the bar the other night said I looked
like an undercover man for the Vatican. It must depend
on the point of view. (*He adds, as an out-and-out gag,
directed at* DELLA) Of course, this particular fella happened to be a Cardinal, that mighta had something to
do with it.
    (HARRY *laughs;* DELLA *avoids it, pouring her ginger
    ale*)

HARRY   How old were the boys there, Del?

DELLA   Howard was a year, George was two.

HARRY   I was lookin' pretty dapper there myself, wasn't I?
Get a load a the spats, hah, John?

JOHN   Dapper.
    (HARRY *turns to the portrait*)

HARRY   What about a little drink to George, then, hah?
What about a little drink to the first-born? First-born,
first-dead, they regretted to inform us. George.
    (*He drinks;* JOHN *drinks, awkward.* DELLA *remains
    still*)

JOHN (*In a mumble*) George.
(*Silence.* HARRY *remains at the portrait, his back to the others*)

DELLA We should be going for Nona soon.

HARRY Plenty a time. (*To* JOHN) You should be flattered, you old sonofabitch. How many people you know would come all that way just to kiss you off? How many?

DELLA Well, I guess you haven't seen the line out in the street: all the way to the corner the last time I looked.

HARRY (*Laughing*) That'd be the day!

JOHN I guess.

HARRY (*Frowning, suddenly*) Yeah, where are they all, Johnny? All the people should be lined up down to the corner to kiss you off? (*To himself*) Where did they all go?
(*Pause.* JOHN *and* DELLA *gaze at* HARRY *for a moment*)

JOHN To absent friends, Harry, wherever they may be.
(*He drinks. Offstage there is the muffled slam of a door and the faint tinkle of breaking glass*)

HARRY Goddamnit! Another one! They think this is some kinda *flophouse?*

JOHN What do you expect, Harry? You live in a deserted building, you're gonna have bums looking to get in out of the cold.

HARRY You think this is some kinda *flophouse?*

JOHN *I* don't think so, Harry, I'm just saying—

HARRY Who *asked* you? Did anybody *ask* you? This is still my *home*! You're getting out of it, okay, but this is still my *home*! I'm not gonna have every bum on the East Side camping out in the halls! *Right?*

JOHN Then get out, you idiot! What are you trying to prove! You want them to put you into the *street?* Go out with some dignity, man!

HARRY Who asked you! You're as good as gone, what do you care one way or the other! This is my *life*! Forty years of it! This is my *life* in this place!

DELLA Harry, Harry! I thought we were going to have a laugh?

HARRY Who left the door open anyway! How many times've I told you to be sure to lock the downstairs door when you come in!

JOHN We going to have a Congressional investigation about who left the door open?

HARRY *You* don't have to worry, it's not *your* home, hah?

JOHN You told me ten minutes ago it was, Harry.

DELLA *Stop! (They are silenced)* He's right, Harry! He's right!

HARRY What's he right ab—?

DELLA What are we doing here? Enough is enough!

26

How much longer do you expect me to go out every day, like a fool, looking for a place to live and afraid I'll find one I can't turn down for some imagined fault! (*Silence.* HARRY *gazes at her, uncertainly. It is her first expression of discontent with his stand and he is unable to deal with it; nor, after a moment, is she, and she turns away.* HARRY *is without words and it seems as though he might almost be embarrassed. Finally,* DELLA *turns again, abruptly, and makes an effort to extricate them all*) Let's bring him out, all right? (HARRY *turns to her, not comprehending*) Howard. Let's bring him out. (HARRY *and* JOHN *exchange a quick glance.* JOHN *moves away, idly, to the piano: it is evidently a matter between* HARRY *and* DELLA. JOHN *wants no part of it, nor, evidently, is he invited to take part*)

HARRY He's probably still asleep, Del.

DELLA No, he must be awake by now, I think. He's probably wondering what—

HARRY (*Gently*) Del, he doesn't wonder. He doesn't wonder about anything.

DELLA Well, we don't know that for sure, do we.

HARRY Shouldn't we wait till after Nona gets here?

DELLA Why?

HARRY Well, no particular reason, just—

DELLA Well, then let's bring him out.

HARRY Why don't we wait, Del?

DELLA (*After a moment, sitting, stiff*)   If you insist.

HARRY   No one's insisting, Del. If you want—

DELLA   No, we'll wait. I just thought since he'll be going
back tomorrow and—

HARRY   We'll bring him out, then, Del.

DELLA   We'll *wait*!
(*Her sharpness stops him. There is an awkward
silence. The clock chimes, once*)

HARRY   Why don't we drop that cockamamie thing out the
window some dark night?

DELLA (*Violently*)   That happens to be the only wedding
gift we have left that hasn't been lost, smashed, stolen or
hocked and it *stays*!

HARRY (*Taken aback*)   Del . . . I was only *kidding* . . .
(*Pause*)

JOHN (*At the piano, singing softly*)   "I don't want to set
the world on fi-yerrr . . ."

HARRY   Sing it, John!

JOHN (*Louder*)   "I just want to set a flame in your heaaaart"
. . . How about this one, Harry? (*Sings and plays, neither
well, but with great assurance*) "Don't swat yer mother,
boys, just 'cause she's old / Don't mop the floor with her
face . . ."
(HARRY *joins in and they continue in unison*)

BOTH   "Think how her love is a treasure of gold, / Shining

through shame and disgrace. / Don't put the rocking chair next to her eye, / Don't bounce the lamp off her bean! / Angels are watching you up in the sky, / Don't swat yer mother, it's mean! / Ohhhhhh, don't swat yer mother, boys, just 'cause—"

(DELLA *is very still, utterly detached, as they continue*)

Darkness

Later. JOHN *is in his room, arrested in the midst of some activity, perhaps, and drinking. He has evidently been drinking for some time and it is hard liquor now. After a moment, he moves to the phonograph and takes the record in his hands. Offstage the door slams closed and* FAYE *appears at the living room door.*

FAYE *is twenty years old, very beautiful, black-haired. She is a girl rather subdued in her manner, gentle and without guile. She smiles rarely, and then with a kind of sweet sadness. Yet there is no air of melancholy about her, merely restraint, watchfulness, the qualities so evident in her mother.*

She steps into the room, finds it empty and listens to the silence for a moment before, from the bedroom, the music is heard—as she hears it, muffled. She listens for a moment, then moves from the living room and appears at the open door to the bedroom. JOHN, *his back to her, is not aware of her presence and they listen together, the music heard now as they both hear it, fully. Finally, she speaks.*

FAYE   Hi.

JOHN (*Turning, startled*)   Hi.

FAYE   Where's everybody?

JOHN   Gone to get Nona.

FAYE   How's Howard?

JOHN (*Removing the record from the machine*) Okay. Asleep. If you can call it that.

FAYE That's nice, I never heard that before. (*JOHN regards the record, nodding*) When did you make it?

JOHN (*Frowning, concentrating, his faculties obviously not entirely intact*) Oh . . . a long time ago . . . During the war . . . We made that the last night before Harry shipped out for the first time. Someplace on Times Square, I think. Big night.

FAYE Before my time.

JOHN Yes. (*He pours, drinks. She watches, but makes no comment for the moment*) How was the concert?

FAYE Wagner.

JOHN Noisy, then.
(*She smiles*)

FAYE When'd you fall off the wagon?

JOHN About an hour ago. Do the bruises show?

FAYE A little.

JOHN Should I stop?

FAYE It's your business. (*He gazes at her again, smiles*) What.

JOHN   You're the only one in this family'd say that: it's your business. And not because you don't care. You're a rare one, Faye.

FAYE   I bet you tell that to all the girls. What's the matter, Uncle John?

JOHN   Matter? Nothing, nothing. You mean this? *(Presenting his glass)*

FAYE   No, I don't mean that.
(He gazes at her again for a moment and she returns it)

JOHN   We all burn in private fires, did you know that, Faye?

FAYE   Do we? *(He nods)* Why?

JOHN   *(Turning away)*   Ah . . . *(As if to say: if only we knew. After a moment, expansively)* Well, it won't be long now, will it, sweetheart.

FAYE   What won't?

JOHN   Your passing from the halls of higher learning.

FAYE   I wish you'd be here for it.

JOHN   What are you going to do with it, Faye, all that education?

FAYE   I don't know.

JOHN (*Passionately*)   You should *know*.

FAYE   I know I should.

JOHN   Well, you've a restless soul, Faye, haven't you. Beneath that calm beauty. Always have had. Restless. (*She smiles only*) What is it you want, Faye?

FAYE   I don't know. Something else.

JOHN   Something else than what?

FAYE   Than what I see ahead of me. Why is that, do you think? (*Touching the bottle*) May I?

JOHN   Sorry. Can't get used to the idea of you drinking. Big girl now. (*He is gone into the bathroom and speaks from there as* FAYE's *eye falls on something in one of the cartons; she reaches in, takes it out: it is a small battered child's stuffed animal*) Which reminds me: what happened to the young man? That all finished?

FAYE   Yes.

JOHN   I thought he wanted to get married.

FAYE   He did. That's why it's finished. (*He emerges from the bathroom with a toothbrush glass, hesitates at the sight of the toy in her hand*) How'd this get here?

JOHN (*Shakes his head evasively, pouring her drink*)   Like everything else, I guess.
(*He gestures, taking in the room*)

33

FAYE It was mine.

JOHN (*Knowing it was*) Was it?

FAYE (*Raising her glass*) To health, wealth and happiness.

JOHN And the time to enjoy them.

FAYE Why *have* you saved all this?

JOHN I used to wonder myself. Proof. Of my life. That it really happened. (*Gestures*) Witnesses: they'll testify.

FAYE (*Presenting the stuffed animal*) What will this say?

JOHN (*Takes it from her*) This? This'll say there once was a child he dearly loved and . . . And that's all it'll say.

FAYE That's enough. And these? (*She takes a crucifix from the wall*) All . . . one, two, three, four of them? Why so many?

JOHN (*Wryly*) To remind me of God, maybe: he tends to slip my mind.

FAYE I think you would have made a good priest.

JOHN Do you.

FAYE (*Nods*) I can see, now, why they called you that, Johnny-the-priest. Do you think you would have?

JOHN Would have what?

34

FAYE Made a good priest.

JOHN I haven't thought about it in some time.

FAYE That's no answer.

JOHN (*To the point*) No, it isn't. (*She smiles*) What.

FAYE I was thinking of two priests at the train station the day I left school for vacation. One had come to see the other off and the one that was taking the train came in and sat down a few seats in front of me and the other one stood on the platform until the train started moving and then he began to wave. Only the one on the train didn't turn around. So the one on the platform finally gave up and started walking away. Just then the one on the train must have remembered and he turned around and started to wave to the one on the platform only, of course, it was too late, he'd gone . . . What we need is some simultaneous waving, you know what I mean? (*She pauses*) The reason I asked if you thought you'd have been a good priest . . . If you thought so, and you really wanted to be one, and they wouldn't let you, I think it would be awful. I think we should be permitted to be what we want to be. No matter what.

JOHN They'd have let me.

FAYE (*After a moment*) Really? I never understood it right, then.

JOHN A story too sordid in its details for the ears of the children. (*Grins*) Not really sordid. Fleshly pursuits and all that. Untimely, perhaps, not really sordid. It would

35

have been all right. Arrangements were made. A probation. In time I'd have started again where I left off. It would've been all right.

FAYE What happened, then?

JOHN (*After a brief hesitation*) I wasn't prepared to be quite so lenient with myself.

FAYE But you were so close to finishing. Why did you do it? When you were so close?

JOHN (*Thinks a moment, grins*) I slipped.

FAYE It was a mistake, you know.

JOHN (*Wry*) So they said.

FAYE No, I don't mean what you did. I mean not forgiving yourself for it. We have to forgive ourselves. Because I don't think we can count on it from others.

JOHN You're too young to be so bloody realistic.

FAYE Oh, I don't know how realistic I am. (*Smiles*) You know *Peter Pan,* that corny play? When I was little they had a kind of hokey production of it at school. You know that moment when one of the characters is sick and she says she thinks she could get well again if children believed in fairies? And Peter Pan looks out to the audience and says, "Do you believe in fairies? If you believe, clap your hands!" I was the only kid in the whole audience who didn't clap. I was seven years old and all the other kids made fun of me for not believing in fairies—or for at least not pretending I did. So after that I believed in fairies every chance I got. It gave me a sense of belonging—as they say, you know? Then it got to be kind of a habit that I never grew out of and now I'm nearly twenty-one years old and I still believe in fairies. Which is okay, I suppose, so long as no one finds out.

JOHN   Why?

FAYE (*Smiles*)   They kill you for that.

JOHN   Do they.

FAYE   I think so. So you won't tell anyone, will you?

JOHN   I remember reading somewhere once that the trouble with secrets is that you lose your sense of proportion about them. After a while you don't know any more whether your secret is important or not . . . Maybe that's why we have to tell them: to reassure ourselves that they're really as important as we think they are.
   (*Silence. He drinks*)

FAYE   Are you afraid?

JOHN (*Wry*)   Of many things.

FAYE   Of dying.
   (JOHN *laughs*)

JOHN   There you go! If there was a bush to beat around, you'd chop it right down! Rare! Christ! I wish I'd be here to see what you'll do with that rareness!

37

FAYE   I might disappoint you.

JOHN   Not likely. And if you did, no matter.

FAYE   Oh, yes. You're the only one I've ever cared about disappointing. Don't you know that?

JOHN   Me.

FAYE   I don't know why. I should care more about Mama and Daddy, about what *they* expect of me, but I never have. It's funny . . . (*She has been moving around the room, inspecting, looking, watched always by* JOHN, *and is at the open door of the wardrobe now, looking into it. She reaches for the top shelf and brings out an iron-worker's battered steel hat*) I never had any idea you'd gathered up so much stuff in here. (*She moves to him, smiling, places the hat on his head, regards him, speculatively. He holds still for it, but unsmiling*) Yes, you look right in that. (*He takes the hat from his head, holds it, regarding it himself now*) Were you happy then?

JOHN   When?

FAYE   When you were doing that kind of work, with Daddy.

JOHN   Why?

FAYE   (*After a moment*) I've never thought of you as being a happy man. I just wondered if you were then, before I was born, doing that kind of work.

JOHN   Yes, I was happy at it. It's good work . . . With the

38

hands . . . connecting things . . . building things . . . I
felt about it the way Harry does . . . being up there . . .
until my fall . . . and my *goddamned fear!*
(He hurls the steel hat at the wall; it bounces, clat-
ters and is finally still)

FAYE   You had a right to be afraid. *(He grins)* You did.
You *are* hard on yourself.

JOHN   You don't know anything about it, Faye! I wasn't
afraid of falling! Not of *falling!*

FAYE   Of what, then? . . . Of what?

JOHN   It wasn't fear of the heights. It was the temptation
that the heights offered, of doing again what I'd tried
and failed to do.

FAYE   What?

JOHN   It was no accident! I stepped off! Do you understand! But I survived it, you see. A miracle, they said, a
miracle, nine months in the hospital and good as new!
Hah! So Johnny-the-priest says to himself it must be a
sign, a sign from the Almighty Crucified Bloody Christ
Himself, a sign direct to his fallen angel! There's a reason,
says I to me, I tried and I failed, there must be a reason,
you must *live* now! But I never found the reason . . . because I never looked for it. I've lived for twenty years
wanting not to have lived, ready to welcome my natural
death when it came. And now that it's on me I see how
much I've wasted waiting for it.

FAYE   *But why did you do it?*

JOHN Because I didn't think it was possible to have done what I'd done to him and live.

FAYE To whom? . . . To whom?

JOHN To Harry! (*Quietly*) To my brother . . . And to her . . . and to myself.

FAYE *What*. What did you—?

JOHN He says I have *nothing*. Did you know that? That's what he says: I have nothing. What he means is that I've flushed all my sons down the toilet trapped in rubber or left them staining a thousand mattresses. He doesn't know! If I have nothing it's because I don't lay claim to what's mine! Well, *I have something*! Should I go into the ground without it, with my bloody conscience to comfort me!

FAYE (*Thoroughly dazed now*) What . . .

JOHN Ah, Faye, Faye! What am I doing! What am I doing to you!

FAYE To *me*? Nothing to *me*.

JOHN We didn't betray him, Faye, it was not betrayal. We believed he was dead, you understand? We *believed* it! For weeks after his ship went down, he was only reported missing and we had hope until the night his friend came, his friend from the ship, who'd survived, and told us that Harry was dead, that he'd seen him go under after the ship went down. He believed he spoke the truth and we believed him, having no reason not to. We walked this house in despair, for weeks, and finally there was no more comfort in words, *none!* When we finally touched it was only some last effort of mine to give comfort and hers to take it, we touched, and wept on each other's flesh for dead Harry . . . who was not dead . . .

FAYE (*Faintly*) Touched?

JOHN There was no passion. Unless grief is a passion. There was no love but our love for Harry. An hour. A brief hour of comfort, nothing more, and we meant nothing more to come of it. And then Harry brought his life through that door with his story of the raft, and the weeks alone, and the washing-up on a beach, the story he's told so often since, laughing, like he laughed at us then for believing that Harry could die before his time. The months passed and you were born and he celebrated the birth of his new child, a special child, coming after he'd given up hope of ever having another. And it was twenty years before she spoke the truth to me of that possibility that I would never utter even to myself, much less to her: that the comfort I'd tried to give her that night was more than comfort. Was life. A life for Harry's imagined death. She'd known that truth and carried it alone all those years and asked help to bear it from no one.

FAYE Mama? . . . *Mama?* . . .
(*Faye, horrified, has begun to move finally, backward toward the door.* JOHN *appears to be unaware of this; seems to be no longer talking to her, but to himself, or to someone else*)

JOHN And she'd *never* have told me, *never*, if I hadn't begged for it. Facing my death and begging her to give me something, if there was something to give, the something I'd always suspected there might be. Not to go with nothing! Nothing but garbage! (*He kicks over a carton, violently*) Garbage! (*Hurls a handful of books. With a cry,* FAYE *bolts from the room; he stumbles after her. She reappears in the living room, seeking refuge. He follows her in*) But do you know what I remember now?

FAYE   Stop!

JOHN   It was *his* name she cried out. In the instant of your being, in her passion, in her grief, it was *his* name, not mine. There's never been room in her mouth for any man's name but Harry's. So did she put his name on you even then? And do I have anything after all?

FAYE   Stop! Please! Please!

JOHN   *I want something!*
(*She stumbles to the door, running, and is gone. He is alone*)

Darkness

SCENE 3

Later. JOHN *is seated at the kitchen table, his head buried in his arms, still. In a moment, the sound of voices, indistinguishable at first. Then* HARRY's *voice breaks through clearly.*

HARRY   Can you still make it up four flights or you gettin' soft from all that easy living?

NONA   Where the hell are the *lights?*
(JOHN's *head has raised, but he remains otherwise still, listening*)

HARRY   The landlord's savin' on the electric! Look at her, she's *winded!* You're outta shape, all right! It sure is *good* to see you, kid!

NONA   How can you see me? Where the hell are the *lights?*
(HARRY's *laughter breaks into the apartment as the door is opened. In a moment,* NONA *appears. She enters the living room, followed by* HARRY *carrying her luggage, a single bag;* DELLA *follows.* NONA *is thirty years old, attractive, obviously well taken care of. She looks around the room like one who has been away for some time*)

DELLA   You've put on a little weight.

NONA   (*Not unkindly*)   You didn't have to say that, you could've gone all *night* without saying that.

43

DELLA   But it's very becoming!
(NONA turns to discover JOHN standing at the kitchen door)

NONA   Uncle John!
(They embrace)

JOHN   I always liked my women with a little meat on them.
(Slaps her behind)

NONA   I'm all yours, lover.

DELLA *(To JOHN)*   Where's Faye?

JOHN *(Evasive)*   Out.

DELLA   Hasn't she been home?

JOHN   Yes. She went out again.

DELLA   Where did she go?

JOHN   She didn't say.
(He has turned away and looks as though he might be looking for a place to hide. For the next few moments, DELLA doesn't take her eyes from him. NONA has taken up the picture)

HARRY   From your Uncle John's archives. This was before your time, kid. That gleam you see in my eye, there, that's you. (NONA *smiles; he touches her hair, gently*) It turned out very nice. (*Then, breaking away*) He's a regular pack-rat! Wait'll you see his room since he started to pack up. Like a warehouse. What're you gonna do with it all, John, you takin' it with you, all that junk?

JOHN   I wouldn't think so, Harry, not much point, is there?
 (*Smiles. There is an awkward pause*)

HARRY   Nona, this thing you see in my mouth, it's my foot.

NONA   I noticed.

HARRY   Sorry, John.

NONA (*Brightly*)   I don't like to be coarse, but I'll sell my body for a drink. (*She takes up* DELLA*'s glass, the remains of her ginger ale, sips, grimaces*) Not *that* drink, however.

JOHN   We have other fare.
 (*He moves quickly to the kitchen, the door swinging closed behind him. The others speak quietly*)

NONA   How is he?
 (DELLA *is about to answer, but* HARRY *interrupts*)

HARRY   What do you mean, how *is* he, for Christ's sake!

NONA   Well, I mean . . .
 (*She shrugs, shakes her head, and is abruptly close to tears*)

DELLA   You mustn't cry, Nona. You *must not*. Do you hear?

HARRY   I told her you shouldn't've let her know, right? Just let him leave and tell her after, isn't that what I said?

45

DELLA (*Stiffly*) Yes, Harry, that's what you said.
(HARRY's *words and attitude belie his true feeling:
he is moved at the sight of his daughter and the
reason for her tears; he exposes it finally, and turns
away.* NONA *recovers herself as* JOHN *enters bearing
a tray with bottles, glasses and ice*)

HARRY Hey! Now it's beginnin' to look like a party!

DELLA Are you sure she didn't say where she was going?

JOHN (*With the vaguest hint of defiance now, a necessary
defense*) No.

HARRY Oh, Della, she's always wanderin' off *someplace*,
she'll be back, it's *early*.

JOHN (*Quickly offering* NONA *a drink*) I think this one
has your name on it.

NONA (*Smiling, vague*) So it does.

JOHN How's Phil?

NONA Oh, fine, fine. Getting fat, though, can you imagine
that?

HARRY The way he used to eat those Sunday dinners
around here, I can imagine it. Lucky you moved outta
town, he'd a *ruined* us. Which isn't to say you haven't
been missed. You've been missed.
(*She smiles at him, turns again to* JOHN)

46

NONA   He was sorry he couldn't get away. He's going to call tonight, though.

JOHN   Good. And how are the children?

NONA   Insane. (*Turning to* HARRY) Listen, what're you *doing* here, anyway?

HARRY   Where?

NONA   In this *place.*

HARRY   Living here, last time I looked.

NONA   You must be kidding.

HARRY   Yeah?

NONA   The whole block's *deserted* from what I could see.

JOHN   He finds it very peaceful.

NONA   Well, when are you moving? It's really dangerous, this.

DELLA   Soon.

HARRY   What do you mean, *dangerous?*

NONA   Well, it *is.* Of course, they're going to evict you sooner or later, you know that, don't you?

HARRY   When I want your advice I'll ask for it!

47

DELLA   Harry!

NONA   Well, all right, Daddy, you don't have to shout, don't shout at me.
   (She is suddenly near tears again. HARRY *is surprised and immediately contrite)*

HARRY   I'm sorry, kid, hah?

NONA *(Forgiving him and apologizing for herself)*   I'm just a little wrung out.

JOHN   It was a bad trip?

NONA   Oh boy, we circled that airport for about *three hours.* Any wonder I'm a wreck? What time does your plane leave tomorr—
   (She breaks off as her eye falls on the wheelchair for the first time)

JOHN *(Following her gaze)*   Three-thirty.
   (But he is unheard)

DELLA *(Not entirely at ease)*   Howard's here.

NONA   So I see.

DELLA   For the holidays. As usual.

NONA   How long are you going to go on with this, Mama?

DELLA   Go on with it? For as long as we can, I expect. I hadn't thought about it. Why?

NONA It doesn't make any sense, Mama.

DELLA To you.
    (NONA *looks at* JOHN, *who returns her gaze, but non-committally; she turns to* HARRY, *who looks away*)

NONA (*Resigned, but gentle*) Well, how is he?

DELLA There seems to be an improvement, a real improvement.

HARRY He's the *same*, Della. (*To* NONA, *less forceful, wearily*) He's the same.

DELLA How can you tell, Harry, you never really look at him.

HARRY I look at him. I look at him plenty.

DELLA You don't see what I see.

HARRY I see what's *there*, Della! I see what he *is*!

DELLA No.

HARRY Goddamnit, Della!

DELLA This is for *me*, Harry, one thing for *me*!

NONA Look, let's not fight about it, what's to fight about?

HARRY (*Quietly, to himself*) Christ.

NONA It's perfectly all right, Mama, if you want—

49

DELLA   I know it's all right, Nona.

HARRY *(To* DELLA, *suddenly, finally hearing her words)*
What do you mean, one thing?

JOHN *(Smiling, forced, to* NONA)   What'd you think, she
was opening the floor for discussion?

HARRY   What do you mean, one thing for you?

JOHN   Come on! Nona's right: it's nothing to fight over.
Right, Harry?
(There is a brief silence: HARRY's *attention is still on*
DELLA, *on his question, unanswered. Finally, he
turns away)*

HARRY   Yeah, right. I'll bring him in.
*(He goes to the wheelchair and wheels it from the
room. A silence)*

NONA *(Gently)*   It *is* kind of pointless, isn't it, Mama? I
mean, he can't . . .
(Searches for the word)

DELLA   Understand.

NONA   Yes, Mama. Even the doctors—

DELLA   The doctors don't know everything, do they. If
they did he wouldn't be the way he is, would he.

NONA   But, Mama—

DELLA *(Calmly, intractable)*   He rots his life away in a
Veterans' Hospital year in and year out and will until his

life ends. A week at Christmas is the least we can do, the least. (*At the door,* HARRY *appears, pushing* HOWARD *in the wheelchair. He is a gaunt man of thirty-seven wearing pajamas and a new-looking robe. His eyes appear to be sightless although perhaps they see. He is very still: what movements he makes are occasional spasms of the nerves and not of his own volition. And he has no hands.* HARRY *stops before* DELLA. *She smiles at* HOWARD *and pushes a lock of hair from his forehead*) You haven't seen him in a long time now, Nona.

NONA   Two years, I guess. Three.

DELLA   You can say hello to him. (*Silence.* NONA, *apparently, cannot speak.* DELLA *turns to her, smiles gently*) He might hear you.

NONA (*With great difficulty*)   Hello, Howard.

DELLA   We got him a new robe for Christmas.

NONA (*Nods*)   Very nice.

DELLA (*She glances at* NONA, *who gazes, transfixed, at* HOWARD)   What do you see, Nona?

NONA (*Not understanding*)   What?

DELLA   Your father sees a vegetable.

HARRY (*Painfully, pleading*)   Della.

DELLA   But this isn't Howard. This is only the part of him

51

that came back with the war still in it, without his
beautiful hands . . .

HARRY (*Quietly, imploring*)   For Christ's sake, Del.

DELLA   This is only the remainder of him, what wasn't
spent by the darkness.
   (*Pause*)

NONA   What do you see, Mama?

DELLA   I see . . . myself.
   (*Pause*)

HARRY   Del? . . . What do you mean, Del?
   (*Pause*)

DELLA   Put him where he can see the tree, Harry. (HARRY
wheels HOWARD *toward the Christmas tree, positions him
there, his face only partially visible to us.* DELLA *turns to*
NONA) He loves the tree.
   (*There seems to be no possible response to that
   statement and silence ensues for a moment before
   the clock chimes, once.* NONA *looks at her watch*)

NONA   You still have that crazy clock.

HARRY (*Gazing at* HOWARD)   I'll tell you something. If I
had it to do again, I think maybe I'd kill 'em both myself
before I'd let 'em go to war.
   (*Pause*)

JOHN   You knocking war, Harry? (*To the others*) Listen
to who's knocking war. Him who volunteered himself
for the Big Fight for Freedom.

HARRY (*Derisive*) The Merchant Marine? That's fighting?

NONA Well, somebody must've thought so, Daddy, whoever it was sank you three times.

HARRY It was different for me!

JOHN It was the same war, Harry.

HARRY I *survived* it! It *took* my sons!

JOHN At least they knew better what they were doing in it.

HARRY What'd they know! Eighteen years old, nineteen!

JOHN Better than a middle-aged man who waltzes out on his wife and children for something that's none of his goddamned business and that all—

HARRY It was my business!

JOHN —he has to show for it is a piece of steel in his spine that tells him when it's going to rain!

NONA He has more to show for it than that.

JOHN (*Derisive*) His *Honor*, Nona? His *Courage*?

HARRY You're the one uses words like that, not me!

JOHN You should have been here the night one of your buddies walked in here and told your wife you were dead.

DELLA (*Quietly*) Stop.

53

JOHN   That's what we did that night, Nona, you were too young to remember, but we all sat around and talked about Harry's *Honor,* Harry's *Courage.* You should have been here, Harry, it was a very uplifting conversation.

DELLA   Stop it!

HARRY   So I wasn't dead, was I? It was a mistake, wasn't it?

JOHN   (*After a moment, quietly, surrendering the issue*) Yeah, it was a mistake.

HARRY   What the hell're we rakin' all this up for, anyway? Del? How about something to eat, then? . . . Del?
   (*She finally breaks away from her attention on* JOHN)

DELLA   Yes, fine. There's some cold chicken, how would that be? Nona, you hungry?

NONA   Starved.
   (DELLA *has started for the kitchen;* NONA *follows, and* HARRY)

HARRY   You didn't eat on the plane?

NONA   Who could eat?
   (HARRY *laughs, throwing his arm around her*)

HARRY   No appetite, hah?

NONA   No guts.
   (DELLA *is into the kitchen.* HARRY *releases* NONA *as she steps into the kitchen and turns to speak to* JOHN, *who remains sitting, very still*)

HARRY   Come on, John-o! Hop to it!

JOHN   Coming.
(But he does not move as HARRY *turns into the kitchen.* DELLA *has taken a platter of chicken from the refrigerator and placed it on the table)*

HARRY   I could eat a dead horse with flies on it.

NONA *(Gagging)*   Swell.

HARRY   But we don't have any on hand, we'd have to send out, so I'll settle. How's Chicago these days? Lotta wind in Chicago, it's a windy city.

NONA *(Smiling)*   I've heard that.

HARRY   Chicago, Del? *(To* NONA, *before the preoccupied* DELLA *can respond)* Last time your mother and I were in Chicago was 1934. Year before you were born. John and I were working on the Walker building that year. We were right there in Chicago the summer John Dillinger got knocked off comin' outta the movie house on Lincoln Avenue. *(*NONA *nods as though she might already know this—which she does—but* HARRY *doesn't seem to notice)* We all went to the movie the next night. It was *jammed.* You know, naturally, the whole town wanted to see where the deed was done. Remember that night, Del? The movie was with Clark Gable and who was the girl in that?

NONA   Myrna Loy.

HARRY   Right! Oh, that Myrna Loy. How'd *you* know?

NONA   I think you've mentioned it before.

HARRY   Oh yeah, maybe so.

NONA (*To* DELLA)   Delicious! What *is* that seasoning you use.

DELLA (*Vaguely*)   Rosemary.

HARRY (*Calling out*)   John! You don't hustle, you're gonna go hungry! (*Laughs*) You know what John said that night, about Dillinger? He says to us, You know what I wonder? I said, No, John, what? He says—

HARRY and NONA (*Unison*)   I wonder if Dillinger enjoyed the movie.

HARRY (*After a beat, deadpan*)   That's the last time I tell that story. (NONA *smiles, affectionately*) He better get in here while there's still something left.
      (*He raises his head to call out again*)

NONA   Maybe you'd better leave him, Daddy.
      (*Pause. He considers this*)

HARRY   Yeah, well . . . maybe you're right . . . It's gonna be a quiet New Year's Eve *this* year, kid. We tried to get him to wait one more day, you know, have a few people in tomorrow night, but he wouldn't.

NONA   It probably wouldn't've been right, Daddy.

HARRY   Ah, it wouldn't kill us to make believe a little, would it? . . . It wouldn't kill us. (*Smiles*) Not like the old days. Remember the parties we used to have when you were kids?

NONA (*A delicate ribbing*) Daddy, you're a party all by yourself. Isn't he, Mama.

DELLA (*With a vague smile, distracted*) I've always said so.

HARRY (*Laughs, to* DELLA) The time Billy Vaughan slipped from the fire-escape and was hangin' out there by one hand? And Alice yelling, Hang on, Billy, hang on! And Billy says, For God's sake, woman, don't stand there screamin', get me a drink! (*He laughs*) Went like *that* in his sleep two years ago, Billy, God rest his soul. (*Takes a wine bottle from a cabinet*) How about a little wine with the bird? Now where the hell is the corkscrew. (*Finds it*) Here we go. (*Holds up the corkscrew to* NONA) Reminds me of a joke which I won't tell.
(DELLA *starts out, the door swinging closed behind her again*)

NONA Probably just as well.

HARRY On second thoughts, I will. What the hell, you're a married woman, right?

NONA I'd better be, what would I tell the children?
(HARRY *seats himself at the table again, puts an arm around* NONA *and huddles. Only the murmur of his voice is heard; the words are indistinguishable. In the living room,* DELLA *stands, still, watching* JOHN, *who finally looks up, in agony*)

DELLA Where's Faye?
(*Pause*)

JOHN Della?
(*Pause*)

DELLA You've told her.
(*Pause*)

JOHN *Della?*
(*Silence. They cannot move. In the kitchen,* NONA
bursts into laughter; HARRY *joins her. The stage
becomes dark*)

Curtain

The second night. After a moment, JOHN *appears at the living room door, wheeling* HOWARD *into the room. He moves him to the tree, leaves him there, moves to the coffee table, pours a drink as* NONA *enters.*

NONA (*Not too kindly*) You're hitting that pretty heavy, aren't you? (*He looks at her briefly and drinks. Silence*) Did you get your reservation changed?

JOHN Till tomorrow.

NONA You so sure she'll be back by then? (*He makes no answer*) We should be out *looking* for her or something! *Something!*

JOHN Where would you start, Nona?

NONA Anywhere! It'd be better than just sitting around *waiting!* How can you all be so *calm* about it? You especially!

JOHN You're not mistaking calm for indifference, are you, Nona? (*He adds*) And why me especially?

NONA (*Distracted, offhand*) Well, you know—you and Faye, she's always been your favorite.

JOHN I had no favorites.

59

NONA (*Smiles*) Listen, it's okay, that's the way families are: I was Daddy's favorite, Howard was Mama's, it's the way families are.

JOHN Where is she?

NONA Lying down. (*Looking at the portrait*) George . . . I guess George was everyone's favorite.

JOHN George had the touch.

NONA I used to hate this thing when Daddy first had it painted from that photograph. I thought it was a pretty corny idea. I kinda like it now. He would really've been something, George, don't you think?

JOHN Yes.

NONA He would've been like Daddy. He would really've been something. (NONA *turns from the portrait to see* JOHN, *wincing mildly, massaging his abdomen*) You all right? (*He relaxes, waves her away and drinks*) Mama says they've been coming more and more often now.

JOHN Did she.

NONA (*After a slight hesitation*) Why are you going, Uncle John?

JOHN I don't seem able to answer that to anyone's satisfaction, Nona, so don't ask, okay?

NONA Try me, I satisfy pretty easy.
(*Pause*)

JOHN   I'm a transient, Nona, all my life. This country has never been in my guts the way it's been in your father's. Or your mother's. The moment he set foot off the boat he belonged here, he owned this country, it owned him. The same with her. Me? (*Shakes his head*) I've lived in this house off and on all these years but, your mother said it, it's never really been my home. Thirty-three years in this country and I've never really unpacked my bags. Do you understand? What's the difference whether I go or stay?

NONA   We could all be with you, that's a difference.

JOHN   Christ! leave it alone, will you, Nona!

NONA   (*After a moment, simply*)   I love you. I don't want you to die. (*He gazes at her; she turns away, flustered*) Is that a stupid thing to say?

JOHN   No.

NONA   It sounds stupid.

JOHN   Not to me. (*Smiles, gently*) And who else matters? (*She smiles*) I won't tell anyone you said it, okay?
    (*She is near to tears. In the wheelchair, a violent spasm seizes* HOWARD *and he slumps forward.* JOHN *hurries to him, raises him up, settles him again*)

NONA   Why do they let them *do* this!

JOHN   What?

NONA   The hospital! Why do they let them bring him home!

JOHN   You're a little afraid of him, Nona.

NONA   He gives me the creeps! (*A silence; then, quietly, shamed*) That's charming, huh?

JOHN   Unrealistic.

NONA   Don't tell Mama, that was a terrible thing to say. (*Pause*) ... Do you think he can hear us, like she says?

JOHN   I don't know. She talks to him a lot, though, all the time.

NONA   Do you think she's all right?

JOHN   Maybe more than the rest of us. (*He adds*) I've been known to pass the time of day with him myself.

NONA   Daddy? Does he talk to him, too?

JOHN   When Harry talks, he expects to be answered back. (*Offstage, a door closes*) Don't let on I told you. About her talking to him.
       (DELLA *appears at the living room door, haggard. There is a silence while she moves into the room; she does not look at* JOHN; *he does not look at her. She sits, lights a cigarette*)

NONA   Did you sleep?

DELLA   No.

NONA You should get some sleep. (*There is no response from* DELLA) You want something? Tea or coffee or something? It's hot.

DELLA Yes.
        (*She starts to rise*)

NONA I'll get it. Which?

DELLA Coffee. (NONA *moves into the kitchen, the door swinging closed behind her. There is a moment of silence,* DELLA *with her head back upon the sofa, her eyes closed,* JOHN *behind her; she speaks softly*) What happens when she comes back? . . . Do we really *want* her to come back? (*Silence.* NONA *re-enters the room, places the cup before* DELLA. JOHN *moves aimlessly, tormented, from the room.* NONA *watches him go*)

NONA Daddy's still up on the roof, he hasn't come down. (DELLA *nods*) Why won't you notify the police?

DELLA You heard your father.

NONA She's already been gone nearly twenty-four hours! She's a missing person! They could *find* her!

DELLA She's all right.

NONA Are you just telling yourself that, or do you really believe it?

DELLA One's as good as the other, Nona.

NONA She could be lying in an alley somewhere!

DELLA Be quiet! (*Silence*) How is Phil?

NONA What do you mean?

DELLA Just that.

NONA No, you don't.
(*Pause*)

DELLA Darling, he's always been your number-one topic of conversation. You haven't spoken his name once since last night unless you were asked.
(*Pause*)

NONA Well, I wasn't going to say anything about it, actually.

DELLA How bad is it?

NONA Pretty bad.

DELLA Are you separated?

NONA In a manner of speaking . . . I mean, we're still in the same house together but we're, uh, pretty separate. Listen, don't tell Daddy, though, okay?

DELLA What happened?

NONA You got a couple days? Oh, listen, it's nothing to be talking about now with Faye—

DELLA You're mine, too.
(*Pause*)

64

NONA   I don't know, everything happened. Among other things, he wanted me to get silicone injections.

DELLA   Get what?

NONA   Silicone injections. For my breasts. It's this new thing they invented out in Hollywood or someplace. For women with small breasts. So that's what he wanted me to get 'cause he said my breasts were too small. Can you imagine? I swear, I didn't know whether to laugh or to cry. I still don't. Married six years and *now* he tells me my breasts are too small (*Wry*) But I guess that's about the usual timing.

DELLA   But marriages don't stand or fall on—dimensions, Nona.

NONA   Oh, I know, I know, it was more than that, it got sicker than that. I don't even want to tell you, it's pretty awful.

DELLA   All right.

NONA   The fact is, he wanted . . .

DELLA   You don't have to tell me.

NONA   No, no, I want to . . . (*Pause*) Well, there're these friends of ours, a couple, we've known each other for a long time and Phil wanted us to . . . well, change with each other. I mean, get together some night and just . . . Well, Janet would go with Phil and I'd go with Richard . . . Do you understand what I'm saying? (DELLA *nods*) It was okay with them, too. I mean Phil and Richard talked it over and then Richard asked Janet and she said okay, apparently, but . . . Well, I couldn't. (*Pause*) Or am I being naïve? (*There is no response from* DELLA. *She goes on with false brightness*) Maybe they've been settling for a trio for all I know. I wouldn't put it past that Janet! (NONA *paces for a moment in silence; it is evident in her manner that she is working herself up to something. Finally*) Do you mind if I ask you something very personal?

DELLA Probably.

NONA Were you ever unfaithful to Daddy?

DELLA (*After a moment*) Why?

NONA I'll tell you why. But were you?

DELLA Would I be likely to tell you if I had been?

NONA You might . . . Well?

DELLA No.

NONA Because you never wanted to be?

DELLA What other reason is there?

NONA Mama, fidelity is very often based on nothing more than lack of opportunity.

DELLA Are you having an affair with someone?

66

NONA   No . . . But I guess I'm about to. I think so, I don't know. I don't know what to do, Mama. He's a wonderful man.

DELLA   Naturally.

NONA   What do you mean, naturally?

DELLA   Don't be dense, Nona.

NONA   Well, but, he really is. He says he loves me.

DELLA   That's a start.

NONA   (*After a brief moment, stung*)   Yeah, okay, I can't expect you to be overjoyed. But I believe him, I believe he loves me.

DELLA   Of course you do. Is he married? (NONA *nods*) And how many children does *he* have?

NONA   All right, Mama, all right! Do you think I haven't thought about all that! (*More quietly*) Besides, it could never come to that, busting up his marriage or anything. Because I don't love him . . . I wish I did.

DELLA   Why?

NONA   It would be a reason to do what I want to do. But it has nothing to do with loving him or not. I just want him, Mama. I've felt that way about other men, but it was never as strong as this time. Is this embarrassing you?

DELLA   No.

NONA   At first I used to tell myself it was because I was
never with any other man but Phil, but I don't know, I
don't think that's the reason, I don't know. Do you think
it might be?
   (DELLA *is completely withdrawn now but offers as
   much pretense as she is able to summon up*)

DELLA   I don't know. I understand that's sometimes the
case.

NONA   I have a friend has the same problem. The way she
solves it is she thinks about other men when she's with
her husband. In bed. She thinks about some movie star
or some guy sat next to her on the bus that day, things
like that. But, that's no way, that's as bad as really being
unfaithful. Worse maybe. You can at least be honest,
right? . . . Did you ever feel like that, Mama?

DELLA   Like what?

NONA   Well . . .

DELLA   Like what?

NONA   Well, with Daddy. When you were young. I mean,
he was the first man you were ever with, you told me that.
So, after you were married for a while, didn't you ever
wonder what it would—

DELLA   No.

NONA It's nothing to be ashamed of, Mama, it's a very natural—

DELLA I've nothing to be ashamed of!

NONA That's what I'm saying, I—

DELLA (Harshly) What do you want me to tell you? To sleep with this man and be done with it? Is that what you want me to say?
(Pause)

NONA (Vaguely) Curiosity? What a childish reason that would be. There must be a better reason than that . . . What should I do, Mama?

DELLA Don't ask me, Nona! It isn't fair!
(Pause)

NONA No, I suppose not . . . You might know I'd make such a big problem out of it, right? Something so unimportant? I mean, there are married women flopping down every day by the thousands for the price of a kind word. But Nona goes to church on Sunday, so Saturday night is a problem.
(Pause)

DELLA (Absently) Are we all like Harry, then?

NONA How like him? (There is no response; DELLA is distant) How are we all like him?

DELLA Walking narrow edges at great heights . . . trying to keep our balance . . . trying . . . (She breaks off, shakes

69

her head) I'm going up to get him. (*She starts for the door, stops, turns*) I wish I could tell you what to do, Nona.

NONA I don't want you to tell me what to do!

DELLA (*Gently*) Of course you do, love.

NONA Well, you brought it up! I wasn't going to tell you at all! God damn it!

DELLA I'm sorry, then.

NONA What did you ask for, anyway! Why can't you say *something!*

DELLA (*After a moment*) Because I'm all used up, love. I have nothing to spare. Forgive me.

NONA (*After a moment*) Phil has always said that one of my big troubles is that I ask the right questions, okay ... but I ask the wrong people. (*After a moment,* DELLA *turns and moves from the room. Offstage the door opens and closes. Silence*) How about you, Howard? Speak right up, I'd be glad to hear your opinion.
  (*She turns away from him and is still. The lights fade to black in the apartment as they rise on the roof.* HARRY *stands near the parapet, facing out. Behind him, the roof door opens and* DELLA *appears, holding closed her coat. The door swings closed.* HARRY *turns to see her, turns away again*)

DELLA Please, Harry, come down, it's cold.

HARRY I'll be along.

DELLA   I won't go till you come with me.

HARRY   All right, then, stay! All right! (*Pause.* DELLA *gazes at him a moment, turns and starts again to the door*) Del. (*She stops*) Stay, Del. (*She stays*) Hey, Del! Remember the snowman? (*She looks uncertainly at him*) Don't you remember? We built it up here that time with the kids! With Nona and the boys, the year we had that terrific snow! An enormous snowman. Right there it was.

DELLA   I don't remember that.

HARRY   (*Gazing at the remembered place*)   Ah. Well, that was one hell of a snowman, it lasted for about a month. (*Turns away. Pause*) What the hell's the matter with her! What the hell's the *matter* with her, doing this! This the kind of tricks she learns at that *college*? (*More calmly*) We'll give it a couple more hours, Del, and we'll call the cops, we'll have to.

DELLA   I think so.

HARRY   Imagine me havin' to ask the cops to go out and look for— Listen, she doesn't have any boyfriends you don't know about, does she?

DELLA   No.

HARRY   I swear, if it turned out to be something like that ...

DELLA   It's not.

HARRY   How do you know?

DELLA I know.

HARRY No, you don't. When it comes to Faye, nobody knows nothin'. Faye . . . she's somewhere else . . . I'm telling you, I'm gonna beat the hide off her when she shows.

DELLA Don't say that, Harry. She wouldn't do this without a good reason.

HARRY *What reason?*

DELLA I don't know.
    (*He turns abruptly and is close to the edge of the roof; pause*)

HARRY Hey, Del, look: remember when we used to see all the way to Jersey from up here? Remember?

DELLA Yes.

HARRY Look at it now, hah? They've cut off our view, Del, they're walling us in!

DELLA They? (*Smiles, gently*) Harry . . . you are they.
    (*A silence: he appears to be considering this thought for the first time*)

HARRY It's my work, it's what I do. (*He turns, taking in the buildings looming around and above them*) Higher and higher, Del! You know what they're talkin' about now? They're talkin' about a building a mile high! A *mile high!* Oh, I'm gonna be on that one, Del, you bet your life! Can you imagine it!

(He gazes into the air looking for the place a mile high. She watches him in silence. The roof door opens and NONA *steps onto the roof)*

NONA   Is this a private party or can anyone get in? . . . I thought maybe I could get you to come in now. Good old Tar Beach. Boy! I remember when you could see all the way to Jersey from up here.

HARRY *(Smiles)*   Yeah, we were just sayin'.
(He turns away, vague)

NONA   Look, let's all go in now, huh, it's freezing.

DELLA   You go along, Nona, we'll be down.

NONA *(After a moment)*   Daddy?

HARRY   Look at the glow over Times Square, Del! Couple of hours there'll be a million people down there.

NONA   A million nuts is what they'll be.

HARRY   Your mother and I did that one New Year's Eve. Years ago. Never again, right, Del? *(Laughs)* I had my pocket picked and she lost both her shoes!

NONA   Women have been known to lose more than that in that crush.

HARRY *(Sweeping the air)*   Take a good look, Nona, while you got the chance! The next time you pass through this town, it might all be gone. It's all comin' down, kid! All of it! Sooner or later.

73

NONA Yeah.

HARRY You don't care, hah?

NONA Should it last forever?

HARRY Who said anything about forever! I don't want forever!

NONA Then what does it matter, Daddy? What's the difference when if you know it's going to happen?

HARRY (*After a moment, quietly*) I wasn't ready . . . That's
the difference . . . I wasn't ready.

NONA (*Logically*) So, you just *get* ready, Daddy. And stop
driving yourself crazy about it. (*Looks at* DELLA) And
Mama, too, from what I can see.

DELLA Be quiet, Nona.

NONA Why? I'm not right?

DELLA You don't know.

NONA What don't I know? (*There is no response from*
DELLA) Well, what? That you're being thrown out of
your home? That Uncle John is going away to die? That
Faye disappeared someplace, God knows where? I don't
have a college education, Mama, but I'm not stupid,
what don't I know?

DELLA You know things, love. There's more to know.

HARRY (*Quietly*) Do you know I killed that kid yesterday? How about that, Nona, do you know that?

74

NONA (*Puzzled*) What kid?
(*Pause*)

DELLA (*Fearful, cautious*) Harry? . . . What do you mean?

HARRY Old man, he says. Old man.

NONA What kid?

DELLA Harry, what do you mean?

HARRY He was needling me since the first day he come on the job. Oh, he was cocky! He looks at me and he says, Oh, yeah, I heard a lot about you, nobody walks the iron like Harry they tell me, I been hearing about you all the way from Seattle, that's what they tell me, all right. So I said, They tell you right, son. I knew he was giving me the needle, I knew it right off. Of course, I'm surprised now I finally see you, he says. I said, What'd you expect, six hands? He says, No, I just didn't figure you to be this old a guy. I said, If you're as good as me, son, you'll get to be my age, too. He says, Oh, I'm good, all right, pop, I'm good, all right. He was, too. But he was always ridin' me, for two months, every chance he got, and I told him to knock it off, I told him to stop with the needle! I *told* him!

DELLA What happened, Harry?

HARRY Well, he was takin' some *terrible* chances, all the time, and all the time ridin' me. Then the other day when I slipped, he—

DELLA You what?

HARRY (*Impatiently*)   I *slipped*. I fell a couple a *feet, for-get* it . . . But he didn't say anything. After they pulled me up, he didn't say anything, he just looked at me—and smiled. Then, yesterday, we were working alone on the eighteenth floor and he was jumpin' around up there like he was on the sidewalk. I told him if he didn't knock it off I'd bring him up on charges, I'd have him thrown outta the union. He says, What's the matter, pop, make you nervous, after yesterday? The old gray mare ain't what she used to be? I said, I'm as good as ever I was, sonny! Oh, yeah? he says. Show me, pop. (*Puzzled, as though he still cannot believe it*) And then it started. (*A moment*) We were alone up there, nobody around. He started doing *tricks*. *Tricks!* Jesus. Walking beams with his eyes closed, walkin' backwards. I'm telling you, he was crazy, this kid! And everything he did, he'd say, How about that, pop, can you do that? And I had to do it. I *had* to. *Right?*

NONA   Jesus, Mary and Joseph.

HARRY   But he was getting madder and madder, because everything he did, I did. There was nothing he did I couldn't match, you see? Then he says, See that beam down there, pop? Watch this. And I yelled for him to stop now, but he jumped for this beam. And he almost made it, but his feet slipped off and he grabbed on with one hand and smacked his skull. Harry! he says. Harry! Save me! And there was no other way to get to him fast enough but to jump it, like he did, there was no other way, so I jumped! And I made it! And I just got to him and reached out and he said, Mother of God . . . and he went.
    (*Pause*)

DELLA You didn't touch him, Harry!

HARRY But if I hadn't a kept matching him, he wouldn't've done it! He wouldn't've tried, it wouldn't've happened! I pushed him *to* it!

NONA (*Furiously*) Some stupid, crazy kid comes along and you have to prove to him how *good* you are?

HARRY Not to *him*! Use your head, Nona! Even *I* know that much! Not to him!

NONA Did you tell *them*, Daddy? How it happened? (*There is no response*) Did you tell them!

HARRY No!

NONA You have to tell them.

DELLA What is there to tell them! He has nothing to tell!

NONA Mama!

DELLA You heard him, didn't you! It wasn't his fault! He didn't touch him!
 (NONA *gazes at her mother*)

HARRY (*Quietly*) Nobody was surprised. They all knew what a crazy kid he was, they knew it would happen sooner or later. If I tell them, it'll be the end of me in this work. The end of me.

NONA (*Calm, insistent*) You have to tell them, Daddy. It's the right thing to do.

DELLA Shut up, Nona! Shut up!
(*Pause*)

NONA Good God.
(*She wheels, and leaves the roof. There is a moment of silence*)

HARRY Del? . . . Don't say anything to John.

DELLA Come down now, love, it's so cold.

HARRY I'll tell you the worst thing of all about it . . . After he fell . . . you know what I was thinking to myself? I was thinking . . . well, *I made it*. He missed, but *I made it*, I'm *still* the best, as good as I ever was . . . That's what I kept thinking, watching him fall . . . How can I go up there, knowing I thought such a thing? And if I don't go up there . . . where can I go? . . . You sure you don't remember that snowman, Del? It was George's idea, I remember that, he said let's make a snowman, I thought sure you'd remember that, that was a great time we had. We had some, didn't we, in this place? Didn't we have some times, though!

DELLA Forget them, Harry. The times we had are gone.

HARRY (*Almost pleadingly*) Don't say that, Del, how can you say that?

DELLA Forget them, Harry! For *God's* sake!
(*Silence*)

HARRY (*Quietly*) I can't.
(*The lights dim to black on the roof as they rise in the apartment. NONA is seated in the living room,*

still, smoking. JOHN *appears, entering the room, glances at her, touches her in passing and moves into the kitchen)*

NONA It's cold in here.

JOHN They turn off the heat early. Like the lights in the hallway. (*Wry*) Subtle attacks on our comfort, encouraging us to vacate the premises.
(NONA *rises and moves into the kitchen)*

NONA Do you know about that kid was killed yesterday?

JOHN Yes.

NONA And?

JOHN And what?

NONA He has to tell them, that's all.

JOHN (*After a moment*) Tell who what?

NONA You *don't* know, then.

JOHN I don't understand, love.
(*Offstage, the apartment door closes)*

NONA It was his fault.

JOHN Whose?
(DELLA *steps into the living room, and stands, listening)*

NONA   His! The kid was making fun of him, saying he wasn't any good any more, then they started having a, I don't know, a *contest*, or something. A *contest*! Jesus!

JOHN   Oh, no.

NONA   Daddy won . . . Now he says there's nothing to—
(DELLA *steps into the kitchen*)

DELLA   Haven't you enough worries of your own, Nona, without bothering with ours?

NONA (*After a brief moment*)   I thought I was still a member of this family. My mistake.

DELLA   What's it to you what he tells and what he doesn't?

NONA   It's the right thing to do!

DELLA   Then be sure you do the right thing for yourself when the times comes!
(NONA *looks at her for a moment, turns, and leaves the room quickly; she crosses the living room and exits*)

JOHN   It's true? (*There is no response*) A contest? (*She looks coldly at him and moves toward the door; he blocks her path*) Did he *touch* the boy, Della? Did he!

DELLA   No! Get out of my way.

JOHN   That's the finish of him, you know that, don't you? They'll never let him work again, never.

80

DELLA   I won't talk about it with you.
(*She moves again to pass around him; he seizes her*)

JOHN   Well, you'll *have* to *talk* about it, woman!

DELLA   Not to you! *Don't touch me! (She breaks from his grasp, wheels, retreats to the opposite side of the room. He stares at her, moves slowly toward the table. As he reaches it a violent spasm seizes him, doubling him up. He crashes both fists down on the table. She whirls, watches, and in a moment it becomes evident that she is not going to move) Suffer.*
(*The pain apparently all but paralyzes him and he seemingly cannot move to aid himself. But, finally, she can stand by and watch no longer. She moves to the cabinet, gets the small bottle and places it on the table while she gets the syringe. Her back is to him when* JOHN, *looking at the bottle for a moment, finally takes it in his hand and smashes it down on the table, shattering it. She turns, startled, and looks. He turns slowly to look at her. Silence. In the living room,* HARRY *appears in the door. He steps into the room as* DELLA *bursts from the kitchen, moving quickly*)

HARRY   Where you going?

DELLA   For a walk.
(*He nods as she passes him and goes out*)

HARRY   (*Gently, but calling out*)   Don't be long! (*In a moment,* JOHN *appears from the kitchen, his hand wrapped with a handkerchief*) I'm gonna call the cops, she don't show soon. (*Silence*) You don't think I should?

81

JOHN   Whatever you say, Harry.

HARRY   What do you mean, whatever I say? I'm asking
you what you think, you're still a part of this family.
 (*Pause*)

JOHN   I don't think you have to call the cops.
 (*Pause*)

HARRY   She don't show soon, I'm gonna call 'em. (*Nodding at* JOHN's *hand*) What happened?

JOHN   Accident.
 (*Pause.* HARRY *stands near* HOWARD *for a moment
in silence, gazing at him; finally he turns away*)

HARRY   (*Jerking his head upward*)   Funny up there, now.
Used to be able to see all the way to Jersey, remember?
I never even noticed while it was happening. Just all of
a sudden, there it is: we got no more view. Minute ago
I was blaming somebody else, Della says it's me, I'm one
of the ones who do it. I never thought about it that way,
you know? . . . You want to hear a real crazy thing, John?
. . . The past year or so on the job I've been having this
feeling . . . this urge, you know, to . . . well, to step off.
You know what I mean? Just to step off up there, into
the air . . . And you know what I would do? I'd do me
a dance, John. I would dance in the air, all the way down.
I see it like in a dream: very slow. You know how in a
dream you fall very slow . . . Like that . . . (*With a short
bark of a laugh*) Wouldn't that be the hell of a way,
John!
 (*Silence*)

JOHN   Harry . . . When are you going to quit?

HARRY   *Quit? Quit what?*

JOHN   You can't walk the iron forever, Harry, you have to come down some day.

HARRY   (*Coldly*)   From a lot of other people I expect that, maybe, not from you. I don't take it from you, someone who should know better. You ever say it to me again, I'll put you through the wall.

JOHN   (*Calmly*)   I'll break at least *one* of your arms first. (*Silence. They meet each other's gaze, neither flinching for a moment. Then* HARRY *grins*)

HARRY   Well, standin' behind a bar all these years hasn't taken any a the lead outta your pencil, John-o.

JOHN   I try to maintain my standards. (HARRY *grins, nods, turns away*) And I'm telling you you should quit.

HARRY   (*Wheeling on him*)   I'll *never* quit!
(*Silence. A sound in the hall is followed by the closing of the door. They turn to the sound as* FAYE *appears in the living room door. For a moment, there is absolute silence, stillness: a tableau is struck*)

FAYE   (*To* JOHN)   I thought you'd be gone.

HARRY   (*Quiet, dangerously so*)   You did, hah? You figured he was just gonna take off, just like that, not knowing

83

where the hell you were or what happened to you? What do you take us for? Get in here. (*She moves into the room, removing her coat*) You know we were ready to call the cops for you?

FAYE You didn't have to do that.

HARRY (*Still quiet, but nearer the edge*) Yeah, well, I can see that, can't I! Where've you been?

FAYE Where's Mama?

HARRY She's out. Where've you been, I said. (FAYE *looks at* JOHN, *and away.* HARRY *misinterprets her look as one of discomfort, a reluctance to speak in* JOHN's *presence*) John? Take a powder, will you? (JOHN *doesn't move*) I want to talk to her!

JOHN Listen, Harry—

HARRY *Will you, John?* Will you, please! (JOHN *looks at* FAYE, *who carefully doesn't return his look. Finally, he moves, there being nothing else to do. He moves through the door and out.* HARRY *follows, closing the door. Silence*) If you don't want what I figure you got comin' to you, you better start talkin' and fast.
    (*There is silence for a moment, during which* JOHN *enters his room, sits and rests his head in his hand*)

FAYE What do you want?

HARRY Now, listen, Faye: don't pull that stuff on me. I want to know where you've been for the past twenty-four

84

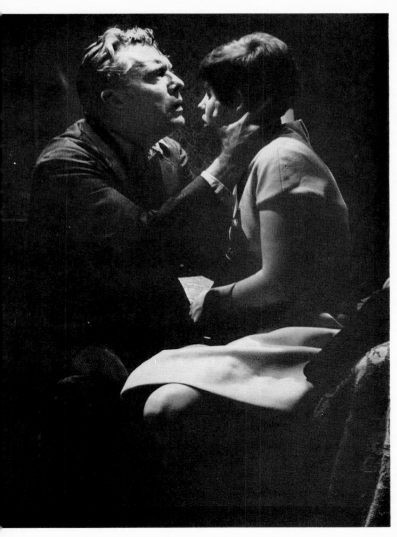

Edmond O'Brien as HARRY and Kim Darby as FAYE.

hours and why. You realize your mother's almost nuts?
What the hell's the matter with you! Now, let's have it!

FAYE   I've been in a hotel on West Forty-fifth Street.

HARRY   What the hell for?

FAYE   Staying there.

HARRY   All this time?

FAYE   I was in a few bars before I went to the hotel.

HARRY   Have you gone crazy?

FAYE   No.

HARRY   Then, what the hell are you *talking* about!

FAYE   You asked where I've been, I'm telling you. Before
I was in the bars, I walked around a lot. But it got very
cold and I started going into the bars . . . Then I went
to the hotel. At four o'clock when the bars closed. This
morning.
   (*Pause. He waits*)

HARRY   *Well?*

FAYE   That's all.

HARRY   I'm telling you now, Faye, I'm gonna smack you!

FAYE (*Reasonably*) I expect that.

HARRY What do you mean *you expect that*? You say that like all I ever do is belt my kids around!

FAYE No, I didn't mean that. I meant—

HARRY I never lifted my hand to *any* of you! Ever!

FAYE I know. You've been a wonderful father.
(*The unintended flattery disconcerts him momentarily; then he becomes, forces himself to become, very reasonable*)

HARRY Now, look, kid . . . I want to be fair with you, you see? That's very important. But you can't waltz outta here and disappear all night and all day and waltz back in and that's that. I want to know what it's all about and you're going to tell me. Where have you been and why?

FAYE I've told you where and there's no reason.

HARRY There has to be a reason! You don't do something like that without a reason!

HARRY Roaming around a lotta bars, staying in some flea-bag of a hotel? Now, why!
(*A pause. When she speaks it is too quick, too glib, too easy*)

FAYE I was very upset about Uncle John and I didn't want to have to say goodbye to him and everything.
(*Pause*)

HARRY   Faye . . . you've always been one with a straight answer, all your life, no matter what. What's happened to that all of a sudden?

FAYE   Nothing, it's the truth.

HARRY   I don't believe you!

FAYE   Believe me. Please.

HARRY   You're lying to me! Do you think I can't tell when one of my kids is lying to me! It's all *over* you!

FAYE   (*After a moment*)   Suppose I am.

HARRY   I don't want to be lied to!

FAYE   How do you know?

HARRY   What do you mean, how do I know! What do you mean how do I *know*!

FAYE   How does anyone know he doesn't want to be lied to until he knows what the true thing is. Everybody goes around saying tell me the truth and you do and they kill you. I don't understand that.

HARRY   No one around here'll kill you for it!
         (*Pause*)

87

FAYE   Everything I said is true, that's exactly what I did, except I was with a man. In the hotel.
(Pause)

HARRY *(Quietly)*   You were what? What man? You were *what?*

FAYE   I don't know who he was, I met him in one of the bars.
(He seizes her by the arms, horrified)

HARRY   *Have you gone crazy?*

FAYE   He gave me money. I found it when I woke up.

HARRY *(Striking her)* Stop!

FAYE   He must have thought I was a professional. Fifty dollars, it's in my pocket.

HARRY *(Strikes her)*   That's enough, now! *(Strikes her again)* That's enough!
(She crumples finally and weeps. Her words are instinctive)

FAYE   Daddy, don't.
(He pushes her away with revulsion)

HARRY *(Almost a whisper) Don't call me that.*
(She has fallen to the floor, turned away from him,

as he stiffens suddenly. He turns away abruptly as though seeking the words in the air, to swallow them. It has taken the moment for FAYE *to hear them)*

FAYE What? What did you say?

HARRY (*Forced, the very banality of the words betraying the lie of them*) You heard me! What man wants to think his own daughter could do such a thing! It makes me want to vomit!
    (*Silence. She has begun to be horrified*)

FAYE (*Very quietly*) You know.
    (*The words fall like a blow on the back of his head and it is a moment before he speaks, wildly, looking for escape*)

HARRY *Know? Know what? What?*

FAYE *You know.*

HARRY I don't know what you're talking about!

FAYE You do! . . . You've always known, then! You must have! . . . Always!
    (*There is a long silence*)

HARRY (*Quietly*) They couldn't last a few more hours? After twenty years, they couldn't keep it a few more hours? What've they done to you, kid?

FAYE (*Faintly, still confused*) Him . . . it was him . . .

89

HARRY (*In despair*) Oh, Jesus, Jesus, so this is what it's all been about. Oh, the bloody fool.

FAYE You know.
(*She shakes her head, not comprehending, weeping now. He whirls on her, seizing her again, but tenderly now*)

HARRY I know nothing! Don't you see, Faye! Nothing! You have to be like me now! *Don't know! Don't!*

Darkness

Later. NONA *is in the kitchen preparing a drink;* HOWARD, *as before, is in the living room.* FAYE *steps into the living room, a bruise on her cheek, a small white bit of adhesive at the corner of her mouth. She attends the noise in the kitchen, but does not otherwise respond to it. She moves to* HOWARD, *takes a small handkerchief from a pocket and touches it to the corner of his mouth.* NONA *emerges from the kitchen.*

FAYE   How are you, Howard?
(*She leans forward and kisses him gently on the forehead*)

NONA   You, too?

FAYE   Me too what?

NONA   I understand Mama talks to him. At length. (FAYE *nods*) You don't think that's strange?

FAYE   No.

NONA   Sending it all out and not getting anything back?

FAYE   Maybe she does.

NONA (*Proffering her glass*)   You want one? (FAYE *shakes her head*) Happy New Year. (*She drinks*)

91

FAYE   I saw a picture of that place he lost his hands, in Italy. Cassino. It's all built up again, you know, the monastery on top of the mountain. There isn't any sign left of the war, it's very beautiful . . . Maybe his hands are still there. In the mountain. Holding the earth.
(A pause. Finally, she moves away from HOWARD)

NONA   How do you feel? (FAYE *nods*) Don't tell Mama I know about her talking to him.

FAYE   Why not?

NONA   (*Shrugs*)   I don't know. Uncle John said not to let on I know, I'm just passing it along. (FAYE *smiles, wryly*) What.

FAYE   Nothing.
(A pause)

NONA   She must be asleep finally, I didn't hear anything when I went by her door just now. I wonder what's keeping *them*? If Uncle John doesn't get him out of Leary's pretty soon, he's gonna have to *carry* him home. That'd be a switch, wouldn't it? . . . He's changed, hasn't he, Faye?

FAYE   Who?

NONA   Daddy. He's different. Even just since I saw him last and that was, what, less than a year ago. I noticed it right when I first saw him last night. He seems so angry. Why is he so angry? That's why I wasn't surprised at all he did what he did to you. Okay, you gave us all a hard time, but he had no right to do that.

FAYE Well . . . the question isn't so much whether or not we have the right to do something, Nona, the question is in whether or not we exercise the right. (*Smiles*) Right?

NONA (*Confused, but putting a face on it*) Yeah, well, that's what I meant. (*She adds*) I guess. (*And adds again*) I didn't go to college (*A pause; she studies the ice in her glass*) Why did you do it, Faye?

FAYE You heard it: I was drunk.

NONA (*Gently*) Come off it.

FAYE No?

NONA A girl like you doesn't shack-up with some strange man she meets in a bar just because she gets drunk.

FAYE What's a girl like me? . . . (*Smiles*) How are the kids, by the way, I never asked, I'm sorry.

NONA Stay single.

FAYE And Phil?

NONA Fine, fine. (*Pause*) Say, have you heard about that new operation, someone invented a way to make your breasts bigger, silicone injections or something? You know anything about that?

FAYE (*Shakes her head*) Why?

NONA I was just wondering, you know, if it hurts or what.

FAYE I hope so.

NONA Well, you can afford to say that, *you'll* never need it.

FAYE Do you?

NONA *Me?* No, *I* don't need it, I was just curious. Phil read about it in some magazine. I was just wondering if it hurts or what. (*A silence while she moves nervously and stops, apparently studying the wallpaper*) So, you're not saying, huh?

FAYE Hm?

NONA What I asked you before, why you did that. You weren't raised to wind up doing something like that. No matter how cool you are about it now, you can't think something like that is right. You have to have a reason. I mean, a moment when you say to yourself, I'm going to do that because, and then you do it. There must have been.

FAYE (*Gently, a realization*) You want there to have been. (NONA's *silence is her admission*) Why?

NONA It's important to me, I guess.

FAYE Why?

94

NONA (*After a moment*) Well, if you had no reason, it would mean that it was possible to . . . go over the edge, break all the rules, just because . . . we felt like it. With no more justification than that. Do you understand what I'm saying? I couldn't bear to think that, Faye.

FAYE Why couldn't you?

NONA I just couldn't.

FAYE You still go to church?

NONA (*Tight, defensively*) This has nothing to do with that.

FAYE (*After a moment*) I did it because I felt like it, Nona. That's the only real and final reason we do anything. All the rest is . . . camouflage. And complication.

NONA You don't believe that.

FAYE (*Flaring*) I believe it! What is it, are you thinking of making the rounds of *your* local bars for a likely prospect and want to know what to tell yourself?
(*Silence.* NONA *is stung, of course, but* FAYE's *words are perhaps too uncomfortably close to the truth to afford any real defense against them*)

NONA (*Quietly*) Thank you, Faye. You're a sweetheart.

FAYE I'm sorry, Nona, really I am, that was cruel . . .
(*Offstage, the door closes as, simultaneously, the*

door to JOHN's *room opens and* DELLA *appears there; she steps into the room as* JOHN *appears at the living room door, his hand bandaged neatly)*

NONA   Couldn't you find him?

JOHN   Yeah, I found him.

NONA   Where is he, is he coming?

JOHN   I lost him again. I went into the john, he was gone when I came out.

NONA   Is he very drunk?

JOHN   *(Wry)*   Well, you can't always tell, Nona: Harry has what's been called an intoxicated personality.
(In the bedroom, DELLA *sits on the bed, vague)*

NONA   Well, I hope he shows soon, it's almost midnight.

JOHN   What're your plans, sweetheart, are we all going to gather round the piano and sing "Auld Lang Syne"?

NONA *(After a moment)*   No, that's not my plan, I have no plan.

JOHN   I'm sorry, kid.
(There is silence, unease in the room. DELLA *has risen and moved to the phonograph; she turns it on and places the arm on the record: the music is heard, muffled: "I Don't Want to Set the World on Fire")*

NONA What's that?

FAYE Mama.
(A moment of silence before NONA *looks up, brightly, bravely)*

NONA Well, I'll tell you what I *am* gonna do. I bought myself a new dress a few days ago especially for tonight —well, last night—and I'm damned well going to put it on right now and if anyone cares to make jokes about it, be my guest.
(She turns and leaves the room. There is silence for a moment)

JOHN I'd ask you to forgive me, but I can't bear to admit to myself that I've done anything that needs forgiving. As shameful as that may be. And if I have, I keep remembering what you said about forgiving oneself. At least . . .

FAYE What.

JOHN You didn't tell him. I knew you wouldn't. She thought you might.

FAYE No, I didn't tell him.
(She rises, moves toward the door)

JOHN Faye! Wait! There are things to be said!

FAYE But, there aren't. That's just it. Not for us. We can't help each other any more. *(She moves to the door, stops, turns to him again)* You were right . . . About the private fires.

97

(She turns and leaves the room. As she appears at the door to the bedroom, JOHN *moves to the kitchen, steps in, the door closing after him.* FAYE *watches her mother for a moment, who stands still at the now silent phonograph.* FAYE *closes the bedroom door. In the kitchen,* JOHN *is motionless at the window. The outer door is heard and* HARRY *steps into the living room. He listens to the silence for a moment, then turns to* HOWARD)

HARRY   They've left you all alone, hah, Howard? Could you use some company, kid? *(In the kitchen, John's head moves, almost imperceptibly, at the sound of* HARRY's *voice)* How about a change of the view, son? Would you like that? *(He moves the wheelchair down near the sofa and* HOWARD *faces out now, his face clearly visible.* HARRY *laughs quietly)* I foxed your Uncle John, Howard. I *told* him I didn't want any company, didn't I? Right? He's probably lookin' for me right now in every bar on the Avenue. *(He slumps into the sofa as though suddenly overwhelmed by exhaustion, rests his head on the sofa-back, closes his eyes)* A change of the view.

FAYE   What will you do with all of this?

DELLA   Throw it away.

FAYE *(After a moment)*   Garbage.

HARRY *(Quietly, his eyes still closed)*   You don't care about time, do you, son. It can't touch you any more, it isn't behind you with a knife in your back any more. Do you know how much I wish I could do that, Howard? Do you know how much?

(In the kitchen, JOHN moves, silently, as though about to make his presence known; but he falters and stops, unable to intrude on this terrible intimacy; forced, as an alternative, to eavesdrop. He sits and is still again)

DELLA   I haven't thanked you.

FAYE   For what?

DELLA   For not telling him.

FAYE   How afraid you both must have been.

DELLA   Not for ourselves, Faye. I don't think either of us were afraid for ourselves.

FAYE   For him...

DELLA   For him to know would be the end of us.

FAYE   Are you so certain?

DELLA   Of course, Faye.

FAYE   Yes, we all know each other so well.

HARRY   It'll be midnight soon, Howard. Another end, kid. Want to look at Times Square, son? (*Switches on the television*) How about that, hah? . . . Yeah, there they are, Howard, look at them! Thousands! See, Howard, I don't turn the sound up, though, that way we're even, you and me: they're screamin' their heads off but *we*

can't hear 'em. Right, Howard? Look at them screamin'
their heads off. And nothing's coming out ... (*He laughs
silently, slumps back again, closes his eyes*) Nothing ...
I know nothing.

DELLA Faye ... this man ... this man you were with ...

FAYE There was no man, Mama.

DELLA What?

FAYE I had to stop his questions, you see? I tried a lie
first and he didn't believe that. Then I told him the
truth and that was no good either. So I had to think of a
lie terrible enough to stop his questions. There was
no man.

DELLA Oh, Faye ... But now he thinks ...

FAYE Yes, well, it doesn't matter, though, because I'm
going away, you see.

DELLA What? Where? What do you mean, going away?

FAYE Someplace else. I have no fixed destination.

DELLA Ah, no, love, no, you mustn't do that, there's no
need to do that.

FAYE Mama, I wouldn't be able to live the way you've
lived. I wouldn't be capable of that.

DELLA (*Vaguely*) You don't know until you try.

FAYE I don't have to try. It's not necessary for me to try.

DELLA Ah, Faye, what have we done to you?
(*She attempts to embrace her but* FAYE *breaks from her grasp, almost violently*)

FAYE *I don't need that.*

DELLA (*After a moment*) I do.

HARRY You see, Howard, I've been trying to remember the last words we spoke to each other, you and me, and for the life of me, I can't. What'd we talk about that last time? I think maybe I don't remember because I didn't know it would be the last time, you see? Because, George I remember and I think I knew that would be the last time we would ever speak to each other. At the train station before he went over. I said, You got nothing to worry about, son, it'll be over before you get there. It was so close to the end, Howard, the war, so close. And the train moved out and I never said goodbye. I remember that like it was yesterday, a cold day it was, I remember. A cold day.
(FAYE *moves, taking her childhood toy in her hands, holding it*)

DELLA John has always said we didn't betray Harry. That, had there been love, then what we did would have been wrong, would have been betrayal. That without love, there was no wrong done. That our act of love was for Harry, not for each other. I don't know. I wish it were true, I want it to be. But don't hate me, Faye, please . . .

FAYE (*Simply*) I love you, Mama. I love you all.

DELLA Then stay!

HARRY Ah, Howard, if only I hadn't slipped. That kid would be alive. If only I hadn't slipped.

DELLA He needs you, Faye. There's so little left for him, he needs you. If you think that to deceive is such a terrible thing it's because you don't understand that deception can be an act of love . . . of mercy. Don't you see how unmerciful it would have been *not* to deceive him?

FAYE Suppose he knew, Mama?

DELLA I told you: it would be the end of us.

FAYE I mean always. What if he always knew?

DELLA (*Wry, sadly*) We would all be elsewhere.

FAYE Why are you so certain of that?

DELLA Don't be foolish, love. Do you imagine *he* would have been able to live like this, all these years, knowing?

FAYE *You* have.

DELLA I had to.

FAYE Wouldn't he?
(DELLA *studies* her *for* a *moment*)

DELLA What do you mean?

FAYE (*Faintly*) Certainties.

DELLA What?

FAYE Certainties. The need for them. To live. The need to imagine them if they don't really exist.

DELLA That's no imagined certainty, Faye. There's no way he could ever have known, you see. I was too good at what I had to do. How could he ever have known?

HARRY She said: you know.

FAYE I don't know.

DELLA No, I've been much too good at it.

HARRY You don't know what I'm talking about, do you, Howard. Should I tell you? I could trust you, you wouldn't tell anyone, would you, son. You wouldn't tell. Faye's the only one who would, you see? She's the only one who would speak it and I think we *all* know that. Because she never had it in her to put anything on, you remember that, Howard, even when she was a kid, she comes straight at you with a straight answer, Faye does, always did, and we know where she got that from, don't we, Howard (*At this,* JOHN, *frowning, begins to attend more closely, no longer with reluctance, unavoidably, but with attentiveness*) The peculiar thing, Howard, is I can never remember when I first knew for sure, and *how* I knew. And that's peculiar, don't you think, Howard? A lot of things, I guess, a lot of times. The way they were with me when I come back from the war, the way she was with me all the time she was carrying Faye, the way she was with her after she was born. And that first time it happened I come home one night when she was a little kid and John was playing with her and I called her and she come running to me and jumped . . . and the way John looked. A lot of things like that, a lot of times, that you don't even really see until one day you see them all together and it's right there. And, one day . . . I just knew, Howard. I just knew.

(JOHN *is transfixed*)

DELLA   You won't stay.

FAYE   Stay? And what would I call him, Mama? What I've always called him? And could I do that without choking on it? (*At this,* DELLA *nearly weeps*)

HARRY   What I'll never know is why they did it, Howard. I'll never know that because . . . I can't ask. It's terrible not to know the answer to a question you can never ask. Do you think I'm crazy, Howard? Do you wonder how I could live all these years like this, knowing? But, you see, the thing is . . . how could I not? . . . I love them, Howard, you see? I love them all.

(*The clock begins to chime as* DELLA *moves, stands for a moment, then slowly moves to the door. The clock becomes silent*)

FAYE   Mama? (DELLA *stops*) I only wondered how you could be so certain when you must know that we all have to do what you've done: come to terms. And we all have our way. And who's to say, Mama, for certain? Who's to say?

HARRY   What I wonder, Howard, is if Faye knows so long as it's never spoken, so long as no one makes the words and lets them out into the air, where they can be felt . . .

so long as no one does that . . . it will be all right . . . just like it's always been . . . Do you understand, then, Howard? (*He moves closer to him*) Do you? (*And closer. In the bedroom,* DELLA *shakes her head, opens the door and exits.* HARRY *gently touches the lapels of* HOWARD's *robe*) Howard? (*He shakes him, gently*) Listen, Howard, do you understand? (DELLA *appears at the living room door and stops there, watching;* HARRY's *back is to her. He seizes* HOWARD's *robe and lifts him, violently, from the wheelchair*) Howard? Do you understand?

DELLA   Harry! (*She rushes to him.* JOHN *hurries in, unseen by* HARRY, *who appears still to be waiting for* HOWARD *to answer, while he hangs limp in his father's hands.* DELLA *supports* HOWARD *with one arm, while she places her free hand gently but firmly on* HARRY, *speaking quietly*) Harry . . . stop . . .
　　(HARRY *seizes* HOWARD *to himself, holds him tenderly, as he would a child*)

HARRY   Ah, Howard, Howard . . .
　　(NONA *appears in the doorway*)

NONA   What happened? (HARRY *lowers* HOWARD *gently into the wheelchair*) Mama, what happened?

JOHN   Nothing, Nona. Your dad's had a little too much to drink, that's all.
　　(FAYE *appears and stands unnoticed in the doorway, the toy in her hand*)

HARRY   (*Brightly, forced*) That's right, that's all it is, everybody relax. (*He looks to* DELLA, *whose concern now is on* HOWARD) I'm sorry, Del.

DELLA   Do you want me to take him out?

HARRY   No! Hell no!

NONA   Is he all right?

DELLA   Of course he is.

NONA   What happened?

HARRY   *Nothing happened!* (DELLA *wheels* HOWARD *back to his place near the tree, his back to us again, while* HARRY, *more reasonably, says*) What did you think? I just got carried away there for a minute. A little too much sauce, that's all. Forget it.

FAYE   Is everything all right?

NONA   Yeah, we were all just standing around agreeing as how Daddy's had a drop or two too much. (*To* DELLA, *who is still with* HOWARD) Are you sure he's all right?

HARRY   He's all right, goddamnit!

NONA   All right, all right, I just thought maybe something happened to him, that's all.

HARRY   What're you so interested in him all of a sudden, you can't stand the *sight* of him! (*A brief silence*) Nothing happened. So, we'll drop it, right? (FAYE *moves, passing close by him*) You all right? (*She nods. He looks at her for a moment, seems about to speak, makes a futile gesture and turns from her. He turns to face* JOHN, *whose*

gaze has been constant and not gone unnoticed by HARRY)
What's with you? (*There is no response from* JOHN, *but*
HARRY *barely waits for one*) What're you *staring* at me
for!

> (JOHN'S *gaze doesn't waver;* HARRY *turns after a*
> *moment, abruptly, and slumps into the sofa before*
> *the television near which* FAYE *already stands,*
> *watching the screen*)

FAYE   Why do people do that?

NONA   Some people'll do anything to get on television.
(*With a gentle irony*) Daddy, wouldn't you enjoy that
more if you turned the sound up?

HARRY   What?

NONA   Join the party, Daddy.

HARRY   There's a party?

NONA   Well, you're not exactly helping it along, are you.

HARRY   What should we do, put on funny hats and blow
horns?

NONA   Something less drastic would do.

DELLA   Maybe it's *not* too late, though. What do you
think? We could call some people, have them—

HARRY   No.

DELLA   What time is it?

NONA Twenty of. (*To* HARRY) Last night you said you *wanted* to have a party.

HARRY It's too late now. (*Declaiming*) The end is *upon* us, kid!

JOHN (*Pointedly*) Or the beginning, Harry.

HARRY (*Looks quickly at him, curiously; then, after a moment*) Comin' from you that's pretty funny.

JOHN Well, I've always been good for a laugh, you know that, Harry.

HARRY What're you needling me for! What's the matter with you, anyway! (*To* DELLA) What's the matter with him?

NONA Daddy, Daddy, he was only making a joke.

HARRY What's he got to joke about! He's a *dead man!*

NONA Daddy!

JOHN Not yet, Harry.

DELLA (*To* JOHN) Stop it! Nona didn't come home for *this!*

NONA I came home for whatever's here, Mama, I'm not made of glass.

HARRY He can't even stick! He can't even finish his life where he belongs!

JOHN Where is that, Harry, where do I *belong?*

HARRY With us! Here! Like always! Where we can be with you! You have to go off and die *alone?*

JOHN What will you want, Harry, an audience?

HARRY That's not what I mean! You know goddamned well that's not what I mean!

NONA Of course he does, Daddy. Uncle John, don't—

HARRY Ask him why he's going! Go on, ask him! He says this isn't his home, it's never been his home! Can you beat it?

JOHN That isn't exactly what I said, Harry.

HARRY Then why are you going? This has always been a close family! What happened!

NONA He has a right to do what he wants, Daddy, leave him alone.

DELLA Will you let go of it, Harry! He's going, that's all!

NONA You mean you're not on *his* side this time?

DELLA *Sides?* There are no *sides,* Nona, what do you think this is! There are no sides!

NONA (*Nodding*) God forbid, in such a close family.

HARRY   What's that supposed to mean? There's not much of it left: don't knock it!

NONA   Not much? Look around, Daddy, it's almost all here, almost all there's *ever* been. What more do you want?

HARRY   Here for how long? Hah? For how much longer?

NONA   You could make better use of it than this, while you can.

HARRY   You're lookin' at the end of us!

NONA   (*Sad, gently*)   You *do* want forever.
(*Pause.* HARRY *appears to accept the truth of it, and the impossibility of it; but refuses to surrender to it. He turns to* JOHN)

HARRY   John? (*He moves to* JOHN, *slowly*) John? (*He embraces him*) Ah, Johnny, Johnny. Don't go, Johnny. Don't go.
(*The clock begins to chime. But for that, there is silence for a moment*)

JOHN   You mean don't die?
(*Pause.* HARRY *releases him, steps back, looks at him, turns and moves away as the clock continues to chime. He turns to it*)

HARRY   God damn it!
(*He takes the clock violently in his hands, raises it over his head*)

DELLA   Harry!

HARRY It *never* worked! (*He crashes the clock to the floor, takes it up again*) It *never* worked right!
(DELLA *moves to restrain him as he stoops again for the clock*)

FAYE (*Quietly*) Daddy . . . Daddy, don't.
(*Silence. All are still.* HARRY, *halfway to the floor, lowers himself to his knees, his hands on the clock; he inhales deeply, once, and it is almost a sob*)

DELLA Go out, all of you. Please. Leave us alone . . . Leave us alone.
(JOHN, NONA *and* FAYE *leave the room in silence. A door closes, offstage*)

HARRY Look what I did, Del. (*He takes up the clock in his hands*) Goddamnit, it was the last thing left and I've busted it.

DELLA It's all right, love, it can be fixed.

HARRY I'm sorry, Del. (*She urges him to his feet; he moves to the sofa with the clock, sits, places the clock on his knees*) Well, it had to be fixed, anyway, right? It never worked proper. We'll get it fixed right this time.

DELLA (*Smiles*) We could even drop it out the window some dark night, get us a new one.
(*He grins*)

HARRY Why does it mean so much to me, Del, that this is the end of us? Do you know?

DELLA Of us?

HARRY   I mean all of us, all of us here.

DELLA   I don't know . . . Maybe . . . maybe because you've lived your life at perilous heights, with nothing around you but air . . . and you need some piece of the earth that will always be there . . . where, if you slip, you can't . . . you can't die from it . . . I don't know.
(Pause)

HARRY   The kid, Del, Nona's right about the kid, hah? I mean, I have to tell them about that. Because I was responsible in a way, and I have to admit that. Isn't that right? *(Silence from* DELLA*)* Sure, that's okay, I know it. Maybe they'll understand, though, you know, the way it was. Of course, like John says, I'd have to come down some day, I know that, but . . . I didn't want it to be like that, though.
(Pause)

DELLA *(Carefully)*   Harry . . . I don't think you have to tell them.

HARRY   You don't?

DELLA   It wasn't your fault, not really, you said so yourself. I don't think they would understand that, they would never understand how it was. It's what you do, why should you risk letting them take it away from you for something they would never understand? And what about that mile-high building? You don't want to miss that, do you?

HARRY   No, I didn't want to miss that . . . Maybe you're right.

DELLA Of course I am. And, love . . . after this is all gone, there'll still be you and me. No one can touch that. No one will.
(*Pause*)

HARRY That's right . . . No one will touch that. (*He looks at the television*) Be midnight soon, Del. Lotta people down there tonight. What do you say, Del, should I be first-foot-in?

DELLA (*Pleased*) Oh, yes, Harry! That would be lovely! We haven't bothered with that in years!

HARRY (*Standing*) Okay, then. What do you say, Howard, you want to see too?
(*He wheels* HOWARD *around to face toward the television. He smiles at* DELLA, *turns and exits as the lights rise on the roof. After a moment,* DELLA *moves to the living room door*)

DELLA Girls? . . . John?
(*She turns back into the room.* FAYE *enters.* DELLA *gazes at her, wordlessly, then turns away, near tears, and enters the kitchen as* NONA *appears.* HARRY *appears on the roof.* NONA *moves to the kitchen door*)

NONA Where'd he go?

DELLA He'll only be a minute: he's going to be first-foot-in.

FAYE (*To* NONA) What?
(JOHN *enters*)

NONA   First-foot-in. The first person into the house in the New Year. It's a custom. We haven't done that around here since you were in swaddling clothes, my dear. Right, Uncle John?

JOHN   Just about.
(He has moved to the door of the kitchen to watch DELLA, *then steps into the room)*

DELLA *(Quietly)*   Could he know, do you think? He couldn't know, could he?

JOHN *(After a moment, carefully)*   How could he know?

DELLA   Faye says . . . *(Shakes her head)* I don't know.

JOHN *(Assured now, albeit somewhat forced)*   Don't be foolish. How could he? He couldn't. It'll be the way it's always been, Del. But better. Without me. Better.
(He waits for some response; none comes. He touches her hair, turns and moves into the living room. NONA *is seated on the sofa, her eyes vaguely focused on the silent television.* FAYE *is seated on the piano stool and, as* JOHN *steps into the room, plays the first few notes, with one finger, of "I Don't Want to Set the World on Fire")*

FAYE   Do you remember that time when I was very little and you played a song for me and when you finished I said: that was a red song, now play me a yellow song? Did you know what I meant?

JOHN   Never have.

FAYE Neither have I.
*(On the roof, HARRY turns, a full circle, looking
upward; upward to the heights)*

HARRY A mile high! What must it be like to stand in the
air that high! And what a dance that would be! *Oh my
God!*
*(He remains motionless, looking upward. In the
kitchen, DELLA stirs, as though she had heard, or
something in her had heard, her eyes focused on the
middle distance)*

DELLA (Softly) Harry?
*(NONA leans forward to the dial on the television.
Sound bursts from it, a sustained roar of voices. After
a moment, Harry turns and starts back toward the
roof door, slowly.)*

Curtain